CHILLY FOR JUNE

The Tale of a Glasgow Family

By

Netta Dawson

A Dolman Scott Book

Copyright © Netta Dawson 2012

Cover design by Richard Fitt ©

British Library Cataloguing Publication Data.
A catalogue record for this book is available from the British Library

ISBN 978-1-909204-04-1

www.dolmanscott.com

Foreword

In memory of my beloved parents Rose Anne and Joseph, and to my family now, and all the others who have gone before me. Deep gratitude to all my friends who have helped me on my journey; my love and gratitude to my husband John and my son Raymond for their help, support and encouragement; and a special thanks to my good friend and neighbour George Hill for doing all the typing and without whose help my words would never have been printed.

Chapter One

I awoke with a start and looked round my room still shrouded in the darkness of early dawn. I was still in that no man's land between sleeping and waking, and the dream that I had just dreamt was still vivid in my mind. I was back in the kitchen of that small flat in Glasgow, lying in the bed set into the wall and watching my mother cleaning the tiled range. It must have been a Friday because my mother always did that job on that day, black leading the oven and using the emery boards on the steel surrounds. After everything was gleaming brightly she would cover the whole of it to keep it clean. Looking back now with an adult's eye it seems a thankless job, because after the next meal had been prepared it did not look much different from what it had been before. But I suppose it made my mother happy for a few hours, so I imagine to her it was worth it.

My mother was a small stout woman with blue eyes and nondescript brown hair. She had beautiful skin that shone with cleanliness and although she lived into her seventies, I can't recall every seeing a blemish to mark its perfection. If only I could say the same.

Looking back I think as children we were very fortunate. The 1930's was a bad time for most people in Glasgow; unemployment was rife and most families had a hard time making ends meet. My father was never in this position; he was an engine fitter in the railway workshops and had never had a day of being idle. We always had good, substantial meals on the table, mostly soups, stews and mince and potatoes. My mother was not a fancy cook but the meals were well made and tasted delicious. We were well fed and our house was always warm and cosy thanks mainly to my mother who rose every morning about 7 o'clock to light the coal fire before the men went to work and the children set off for school. We were warm, well fed and most importantly we knew we were loved. Not many children in those days were so fortunate. My father was a nice man and like so many Glaswegian men of that time he liked his drink - or his dram as it was called then - but only at the weekend, Friday and Saturday. I don't suppose he could afford that luxury during the week. On Friday night, which was pay night, all the children would get a bag of sweets and a penny each to spend. You could get a lot for a penny in those days. If my father was feeling a bit flush, my mother would get a box of chocolate liqueurs, which were her favourite.

Glaswegian men liked to think of themselves as macho, although that word had not yet entered our vocabulary. But my father had a gentle side and was very emotional, especially where children were concerned. Any tragedy concerning children would make him weep. He also wrote poetry in his spare time. There was one poem in particular about losing his hair, which had happened to him in his early 20's. My mother told me that when this happened he refused to go anywhere where he had to remove his hat. He even stopped going to church because of it. My mother said that he had had a lovely head of black hair which was his pride and joy, and it was a dreadful blow to him when he lost his hair so early in life. She said it was due to Bright's Disease which I had never heard of, but I suppose it must have been a form of alopecia. I can only remember the last two lines of his poem which went 'The sunshine of my life has gone, my lamp is nearly out.' My father was very clever with his hands and would spend hours making something or another. He was especially good at working with wood. He made a beautiful book case with a fluted top which stood in our living room for years. He even made a cot for my young sister's doll. After my sister Chrissie grew up and got married, the same cot was used for each of her six children. When it was no longer required by her she passed it onto her friend still in good condition.

All the doors in our house were varnished to a lovely gloss. On top of all these jobs he also mended our shoes when they were in need of repair. He had a set of cobbler's lasts of various shapes and sizes. When he had extra time on his hands he made toy soldiers for the boys. We used to watch in fascination as he heated the brass in a crucible over the flame then poured the molten liquid into the moulds. When the liquid was cold he would turn out the moulds and hey presto: toy soldiers. He also had a mould that made soldiers on horseback. One evening when he was not engaged, a friend of my young brother Peter who was in the house at the time had watched the performance with wide-eyed wonder and was gazing longingly at the finished product. When my father noticed him he asked if he would like some soldiers too. 'Oh yes, Mr. Dawson' he replied. My father then asked if he had any brothers who would like them. 'Yes,' said the little boy. 'I have six!' I don't think my father ever made that mistake again.

Another one of his talents was cutting hair. Fortunately, my mother demanded that only the boys suffered this ordeal as they usually ended up looking like skinned rabbits - and not very pretty bunnies at that.

My mother had nine children, but three of them had died before I was born. Two of my sisters, May and Lizzy, died within days of each other in the flu epidemic after the First World War. My brother James died nine months later from pneumonia. My father had wept so much at the death of his girls that he had no tears left to shed when his first-born son died. My mother said that a big lump came up on his neck due to grief that he could

3

not express. With three deaths in a year my parents were distraught and had now the added worry about how they would be able to pay for another funeral as there was now no insurance money left. My father's sister Mary had been saving up for her wedding due in a few months' time, but seeing my parents' despair had offered to give them her savings to help them out. My mother said that she and my Aunt Mary had never been very close but she never forgot her kindness at this tragic time in their lives. A pauper's funeral would have cost them so much shame and anguish. My family now consisted of two older brothers, Joe and John, an older sister Annie, a younger brother Peter, and Chrissie, the baby of the family, two years younger than Peter and five years younger than me.

In the hot days of summer there was so many things to do; playing games of hide and seek, kick the can, and ball games like rounders. And of course for the girls there were skipping ropes. The days never seemed long enough and we had to be dragged protesting up to bed at night. On the really hot days there was a water truck that used to come round the city spraying water on the dust and the grime of the streets. We used to run behind it, letting the cool water run over our hot and dusty skin. Oh the bliss of that cold water, reviving and refreshing us! In the winter we always had snow fights, and we played with our girds, rolling them around the streets and keeping them under control with our iron cleeks. When darkness fell we would sit on the stairs outside our house and when the lamp lighter had lit the stair lights we would tell ghost stories, shivering with a mixture of fear and joy at the scary bits.

Christmas time was a joyous time of the year for us, dreaming of what presents Santa Claus would bring us and hoping he had read all the begging letters we had sent to him up the chimney. At the top of our road there was a Singer's sewing machine shop and every

4

Christmas they had a Christmas club where you could save a few shillings to help buy presents for the big day.

They had a big display of dolls in their window and when Christmas was near they would dress them in beautiful gowns which were made on the premises. My mother always saved up via the club so she would have a few extra shillings to spend on presents. I wasn't much of a girly girl and dolls were not one of my favourite things, although I did like my black doll which my parents had bought me when I was younger. I think I liked it because it was black and different from the blonde ones that most little girls loved. My little sister Chrissie wanted a doll, so my mother bought her one for Christmas from the money she had saved in the club. Chrissie named her doll Gloria and took her everywhere, even into the bed that we shared. Gloria was the bane of my life and I hated her with a vengeance. When I tried to turn over in bed more often than not I would come up against her cold, hard porcelain face and would awake with a start! She was to me a pest and a cuckoo in my warm little nest.

On Christmas morning my older brother Joe had got the bike that he had been longing for and being in a benevolent mood had offered to take Gloria the doll a ride up and down our hall. Unfortunately he crashed into the wall; Gloria fell off the bike and landed with a crash onto the hard floor! There wasn't too much damage done to either Gloria or the bike but Chrissie was in tears and Christmas day was spoiled for everyone! Drat! That blasted doll!

I think that she must have been accident prone as she had another disaster a few days later. My father had bought us a dart board and hung it on the back of the room door. We were all throwing darts with more enthusiasm than skill when one whizzed through the air and pierced Gloria's nose. I got the blame for it and a slap from my mother. When I protested my innocence my mother said if I had not been guilty that time the slap would serve for the next time I was. I suppose there was some logic in that somewhere.

If Christmas was for the children, New Year was for all the family. At the first stroke of midnight the bells would ring out and the ship hooters would sound to herald the start of a new year. Traditionally you had to have a 'first foot', preferably somebody tall and dark and a man. They had to have a gift of food and drink in their hands as this ensured that the household would never be short of these items in the coming year. My brother Joe used to do the honours as he fitted all the necessary conditions. He would stand outside the door for a short time before midnight and as soon as the bells rang out he would come in carrying the required articles: a lump of coal to ensure we always had a fire, and something to eat and drink. After this we all had a drink to bring in the New Year; whisky for the men and blackcurrant wine for the children. We would then sit down to dinner, which was always steak pie, potatoes and vegetables. Staying up so late was a great treat for us children. It was the only time in the year that this happened. After a short time the neighbours and our friends would appear and we would have a party until the early hours of the morning. Everyone had to do a party piece and my father always sang 'The star of Rabbie Burns', but changed it to 'Rosie Burns', Burns being my mother's maiden name. My mother would say he was a silly old fool, but I think she liked it just the same. These were the happiest days of my life, feeling secure and safe in the midst of my family. If only these moments could last forever.

When I was 11 years of age, I fell ill with scarlet fever. I had always been a healthy child but suddenly I felt depressed and out of sorts. My throat hurt and I lost my appetite. My mother dosed me with hot lemon drinks and aspirin, but nothing seemed to help. My throat became so painful that I could not swallow any food and I was burning up with fever. After a few days my parents decided to call in the doctor. When he came he took my temperature which was 104 degrees, looked at my throat and said I would have to go to hospital. I was taken to Ruchill Fever Hospital and was there for over a month. That was the loneliest time of my life. My parents were not allowed to visit because of the risk of infection and they could only stand at the window of my ward and wave to me. Everyone at the hospital was very kind to me but I never felt so alone in my life. When I finally came home my mother could not believe how thin and pale I had become. I had always been sturdy and rosy-cheeked, but now I was pale and gaunt, a shadow of my former self. My only worry now was about my 11-plus exam results. I had sat my exam just before I took ill but did not know what mark I had achieved. I wanted to go to Garnethill Convent School where some of my friends were going, but I need to get top marks to get there. My mother went to the school to find out how I had done in my tests and thank heavens I had made it with a 90% average. What a relief.

In the previous year we had been allocated a new house so we moved from Springburn to Possilpark, another suburb of Glasgow. We now had three bedrooms, a lounge, bathroom and scullery. No more tin baths in front of the fire on Friday nights. There was a family called Nelson who lived just up the road from us. They were a young couple with a little girl of five years called Patricia and a new baby.

At Garnethill we had a separate block which housed the school beginners and Mrs. Nelson wanted her little girl to go there. It was decided by my mother and Mrs. Nelson that I should take Patricia to school until such times that she could make the journey by herself. I did not really mind, not that it would have mattered if I had because we did what we were told to do in those days. I used to look forward to going to the Nelson house in the mornings. There was always a cheery fire burning and the unmistakeable smell of Johnson's baby powder and warm milk, a lovely combination. I can still sense this as I write.

I don't think I was a very attractive child at this time of my life. My young sister Chrissie was the beauty of our family with lovely fair hair and big brown eyes. My mother said that when Chrissie was a baby people used to stop her in the street to remark what a beautiful child she was. My hair was quite straight and dark and never looked very tidy and my clothes seemed to hang on me as I was so thin. I was also a bit moody and very introspective, only happy with my nose in a book and lost in my own little dream world. I had joined the library and my favourite books were tales of girls' boarding schools where they would have midnight feasts in the dorm, pillow fights, and visits to the tuck shop to buy all kind of goodies.

We had a small tuck shop in Garnethill and each morning my mother would give me a penny to spend there. I always bought the same things: an Ayton Sandwich and a Rhumba Wafer. The Ayton Sandwich was a rectangular biscuit with chocolate on one side and a creamy chocolate centre. The Rhumba Wafer was a crisp wafer with a coating of crisp chocolate which melted in your mouth. With a glass of milk this sufficed to quell the hunger pains until lunch.

Chapter Two

In 1938 there were quite a few teachers at Garnethill Convent School. The one who taught us history was very tall and had a mass of red hair. We called her Belisha Beacon. The one who tried to teach us maths was small and dainty and she was known as Minnie Mouse. The French teacher was always 'Mademoiselle'. My favourite was Miss Matheson who taught English. She was a born teacher who could make the most prosaic sentence sound like poetry.

At that time there was a comedy strip in the daily paper called 'The Adventures of Rupert The Bear' and every morning Miss Matheson would read us the latest episode. After all these years I can still see her in her black gown, standing in front of our class and smiling at us. So serene, so gracious and so loved.

Minnie the Mouse was the other side of the coin. She may have been a whizz kid at maths but when she put an algebra problem for us to solve she would then proceed to solve it herself and leave her bewildered class trailing in her wake. I never really got to grips with algebra and I put the blame for that firmly on her shoulders.

Mademoiselle taught us French and a little German. I liked the French lessons and had a quite a good accent for it. Mademoiselle said that Scottish children seemed to find the accent easy to imitate! Ooh la la!

There was also a gym mistress who was young and attractive and very nubile. She had us jumping over the horse, climbing up the wall frames and running around the gym like demented souls. I approached each hurdle with great determination, so much so that the teacher used to say, 'Relax my girl, you are supposed to be enjoying this.' I can only say that her idea of fun was certainly not mine.

Academically I did quite well at school. Well enough to keep my teachers happy at least. And the years passed happily enough until all at once I was 14 years of age and ready to be turned out into an unsuspecting world of work. This was the usual age when school days were over for ordinary working class children. We never thought about college or university; they were a prize beyond our reach and our parents' pockets. My two brothers Joe and John were only apprentices learning a trade and their wages were low and barely enough to keep them in food and clothing. So my father was the main wage earner and my mother had a difficult job making ends meet. My older sister Annie had married by this time and moved out to a house of her own, so that was one wage packet less for the family budget.

My first job was only a temporary one, helping out at one of the big department stores for the Christmas period which was only a few weeks away. I thought this was quite a good idea, like dipping your toe in the water before you dived into the deep end. I duly applied for the post and was given a time for my interview. My mother came with me as was the usual custom at that time. I was given a test paper with a few simple sums and answered a few personal questions and then was told to start on the following Monday. The hours were 8am till 6pm with a half-day on the Tuesday when you finished at 1pm. The wages were eight shillings - 40 pence these days. Not exactly a king's ransom, but beggars can't be choosers. I don't think I slept much on the Sunday night due to a mixture of fear and excitement at stepping out into the great unknown territory of the working world.

On my first day at work I was not allowed to serve any customers. Instead I was put in the care of one of the older assistants whose job it was to show me the ropes. I was taught how to write out the sales slip and how to send the cash to the cashier's office. At the end of each counter there was a contraption shaped like a stove pipe. There was small container on a ledge beside it. When you served the customer you wrote out a sales slip and put that and the money provided into the container which you unscrewed to open. You then closed it, pushed it up the tube and sent it on its way along a series of small rails that went all round the shop walls before it was whisked through to the cashier's office. In reverse order it came back with the sales receipt and the correct change to the counter with a loud plop to let you know of its arrival. I thought this was very ingenious, although it seemed that this was common practice in the bigger stores. My mother did not use the big stores very often; she mostly shopped in the myriad of small shops in our area which supplied most of her needs.

My first day passed uneventfully but on the second day disaster struck. I was serving a lady who wished to buy a child's red bike. I duly trotted off to the stock room, found the container labelled red bikes and brought it down to the customer. As I was handing it over, prior to writing the sales slip the older assistant who was my minder asked if I had checked the contents. Of course I had not thought of that and when the carton was opened there were two red bikes instead of one. I was reprimanded and told to be more careful in future as my mistake would have cost the store one bike. Well, how was I to know that red bikes came as twins? By this time it was close to my lunch break so I went home in floods of tears and told my mother what had happened. She was kind and sympathetic, but when I said I was not going back to the store she was quite firm and said that I couldn't let one mistake cost me my job. She came back with me to the store where she took me to apologise and promise that I would be more careful in future. I was mortified, but of course I did what I was told to do, and my boss said that everyone made mistakes when they were new to a job and this incident would be forgotten and forgiven. I worked there until Christmas was over and quite enjoyed my time there. It was the custom in Glasgow at that time that a worker always kept their first pay packet and true to tradition my mother let me keep mine. I spent the money on buying small presents for the family and felt very proud of myself in being able to do so.

My second job was at a small store in Port Dundas about a mile away from my home. It was a sub-post office and sweet shop combined. Miss Kelly was the sub-post mistress and I was the assistant in the sweet shop. This was the time I had my first crush on a boy. There was a railway workshop just up from the shop and quite a few boys from there came into the shop in their lunch hour to buy sweets. At that time there was a popular sweet called a macaroon bar and the firm had a special offer going at that time. The ordinary bar had white icing in the middle but in each box there were one or two with pink icing and if you managed to get one of these you got a giant bar free.

The boy that I liked used to buy one of these every day but never managed to get a pink one. He always looked so disappointed so I thought I would help things along a little. When the boss was not paying me any attention I used to scrape a little of the corner with my thumbnail, just enough to glimpse the icing underneath. I managed to unearth a pink one eventually and put it aside for him. When he next came into the shop I sold him the coveted pink bar and the resultant prize. The joyful look on his face made it all worthwhile. Of course there was no romance or anything like that; I was only 14 years of age. But I was pleased to have done something for him. The innocence of young love.

These little jobs were only a stopgap till I could find something worthwhile and with some prospects for the future. A few weeks after I left this job I met one of the girls who used to come into the shop and was shocked to hear that Miss Kelly my boss had committed suicide. She was only in her late 30's or early 40's. It was a dreadful tragedy. When I worked there I learned a little about her private life. She lived with her elderly mother and had only one relative - a sister who lived and worked in America. Her mother was quite frail, so once a week I used to be sent to her home to do a bit of shopping for her and anything else that needed to be done in the house. She was a nice old lady but like her daughter a very private person. She died a few weeks later and Miss Kelly was in a dreadful state of shock and grief. She had few friends and was very lonely with her mother gone, so her sister agreed to come over for a short visit to keep her company. She told me that she did not know how she would manage to cope when her sister returned to America. My informant told me that when the sister did return to America Miss Kelly went completely to pieces and lost interest in everything. One day she told the girl who had taken my place when I left to go to the chemist for a bottle of Lysol. This was a very strong disinfectant and not sold for general use. In fact it had to be signed for in a poison book, but Miss Kelly had told the girl to say it was to remove some bad stains on the floor of the shop. The assistant in the chemist shop knew Miss Kelly and duly handed over the bottle of Lysol. A few moments later she heard terrible screams and going into the back shop she found Miss Kelly rolling in agony on the floor. She phoned for the doctor but when he arrived there was nothing he could do and she died in agony. What a way to go and what a shock it must have been for that young girl. There but for the grace of God a few weeks earlier it could have been me that found her.

The Cooperative Society was a flourishing concern in Glasgow and had stores all over the city with hundreds of members. My mother was one of these and had been for quite a few years. She belonged to the Co-op Womens' Guild and went to their meetings every Monday evening with one of our neighbours. The basic idea was that each member was considered to be a shareholder and was entitled to a share of any profits made by the society. When you joined you were issued with a share book with your name and share number marked on it and you used this number every time you shopped in the store. Your account had to be paid every quarter and the dividend of 10% of your purchases were paid to you at that time. This was a good method of saving and if you were a daily shopper you could be the recipient of quite a few pounds each quarter which was a godsend to most people. As I was not 15 years of age and had a bit of experience in shop work my mother suggested I should send in an application for a job in one of the stores. So I did so and got a date for an interview at the head office. There was the usual test paper with a few personal questions and a few sums. I was asked if I belonged to any youth organisation. I had joined the Girl Guides a few years before and was now a Patrol Leader. That seem to please the examiner as she nodded her head in approval. Dib Dib! I was told to start the following week as cashier in one of their butcher shops in Maryhill, about 15 minutes walk from my home.

My boss was a Mr. Swan and he was a lovely man and very kind and helpful to me. The shop was not a very busy one and there were times when I did not have much to do, so he suggested that I bring a book to the shop which I could read when there were not many customers around. Needless to say I jumped at the chance. Most of the Co-op shops were in blocks of three: butchers, dairy and grocers. Some also had a shoe shop. I loved my job and soon settled in, but my sense of security and well being was not to last long.

As part of my job I had to make up the bank money each week and Mr Swan would take it and pay it into the account at the local bank. A few weeks after I started I did this job as usual on the Friday morning and handed the money over to Mr Swan who seem to be his usual affable self. A few hours later, however, someone came from the head office and started to check the register and look through my cashbooks and ledgers. It later transpired that Mr Swan had not gone to the bank, but had used the money to pay off debts that he owed. He had gone to the head office immediately and confessed, so no blame was attached to anyone else. I was so glad the society did not want to make a court case of it but of course he was dismissed with no references. No one knew why he had acted why he did but I for one was very sorry to see him go, and in such a way.

His replacement arrived in a few days time. He was small man with a rat-like face and a sneering expression. I disliked him at first sight and even more so when I got to know him. Like a lot of small men he made up for his lack of inches with a lot of bombast. He was very sarcastic and found fault with everything and everybody. What a difference between him and easy-going Mr Swan.

The only bright spot on the horizon was that our yearly outing was only a few weeks away. Every year all the staff of the Co-op were taken out to a popular resort where there were races, games of all kinds and all the fun of the fair. This was my first trip with them and I was really looking forward to it. The great day arrived and we were taken by coach to the seaside. The first thing on the agenda was the racing, so after we had something to eat and drink the applicants for each race got ready. I had put my name down for all the different events: the half-mile race, three-legged race and the obstacle race. I was quite a good runner in those days because I got plenty of experience running everywhere since I was usually late starting out.

There were heats for the half-mile race and I won the first heat beating the other two applicants. And then there was the final which I won also. In the three-legged race I was fortunate enough to be paired with someone who was a very good runner and we romped home in first place and also in the final. To be honest, I was one of the youngest contestants and that gave me the edge over the rest. I made it a hat-trick by winning the obstacle race as well. So it was a good day for me and I felt really proud of myself. There were prizes for the winners of the heats and the finals and you were allowed to pick your prize from an assortment of goods made by the Co-op factory warehouse. I went home with a tie and sock set for my father, a toiletry set for my mother and best of all a beautiful soft-top holiday case which was the first prize for the winner of the half mile race. Not bad for a day out which cost the employees 9 pence each and that included your meal.

Every month every store received a magazine with all the news of the events of the past month and of course in that month's issue was all the news about the outing. My name appeared four times and everyone was congratulating me, even my bad-tempered boss Mr Lorimer. I think he was pleased because his store had been mentioned and he was basking in reflective glory. I will never be famous but at least I got my name in print once.

Chapter Three

Glasgow at that time was a divided city, not by walls or barricades but by religion. Scotland had always been predominantly protestant. At that time of the potato famine in Ireland hundreds of people had emigrated to Glasgow, settled there and raised their families, most of whom were catholics. So there was a large contingent of them in many parts of Glasgow. Discrimination raised its ugly head in many areas of life but most especially in the job market. It affected me twice when I had applied for a job. Everything was fine until the last moment when you were asked about what school you had attended. This was their insidious way of finding out what your religion was. The question was never asked outright whether you were catholic or protestant, but the result was the same. In both instances when it happened to me I had been told that I was perfect for the post, told of the hours and wages and then just as I was leaving came the question about the school. I was then told that they would be in touch with me but of course this never happened. I heard later that this was commonplace at this time. Of course it could never happen in these days with all the laws on discrimination. At that time we had to just grin and bare it.

I have mentioned before about my father's job in the railway. His wages were not high by any means but there was a few perks attached to it. Two of these were privilege tickets and railway passes. With the privilege tickets, which were unlimited, you could travel to any of the resorts on the Clyde for a much-reduced rate. And with the passes you were allowed to travel by train and boat further afield, but you were only allowed one pass ticket in a year. My father had a cousin Maggie who lived in a little cottage in Killyleagh in County Down, Northern Ireland. We had been there before and we loved it, so it was decided to go again that summer for our holidays. We were all delighted and very excited about the trip. The journey consisted of a train journey to Stranraer, a boat trip to Larne and then the bus to Killyleagh which was about 20 miles from Belfast. The only drawback was that the train arrived in Stranraer in the late evening and the boat did not sail until 6 o'clock in the morning. The railway pass did not cover the cost of a separate cabin, so we had to sleep as best we could on board on the hard benches on the deck. My mother and father were good travellers but unfortunately this could not be said about their children, especially my younger brother Peter and myself. The boat crossing to Larne was the worst part of the journey as the North Sea was certainly not a duck pond and we were all seasick for most of the time on board. The bus trip was not much easier as it was a very bumpy ride on the country roads. We were a washed-out lot when we finally arrived at our destination.

My Aunt Maggie lived in a little cottage in the middle of the village with her son and daughter. There were three small rooms, a kitchen and a loft where we four children were to sleep in makeshift beds. There was a lovely smell of apples because the attic was where the fruit was stored after it was picked from the trees in the orchard.

There was quite a large plot of land in front of the house where the potatoes and vegetables were grown and few flowers planted. Of course there was no inside toilet, just a wooden box seat with a big hole in the centre and with a burn running underneath. I was a bit scared of using this contraption; in my imagination I always wondered what would happen if I fell through the hole and was swept away by the burn.

There was no electricity, only oil lamps to provide light. But we loved it. When the lamps were lit in the evening and the big peat fire was burning it was cosy and welcoming. The church was about three miles away and my Aunt Maggie made sure we all got to church on Sunday. When we complained about the long walk she would say, 'Ah sure, it is only a stretch of the legs!' There was one thing for sure: her legs did not get very much stretching, because I never saw her going to church the whole time we were there.

She used to bake soda bread on a big wooden skillet and it tasted delicious, with loads of butter and a home-made jam. We had potatoes just fresh from the garden and glasses of milk straight from the dairy. It was plain food, but so fresh and delicious. The weather was kind to us and we spent all day outdoors, walking in the countryside and playing in the fields.There was a pump in the middle of the village and we used to collect buckets of water for the household needs and to save Aunt Maggie stretching her legs. It was a wonderful holiday and we were all sorry when it was time to return home.

By the way, I forgot to say that this was the first outing of my new case, the one that I won at the running on the work's day out previously. It certainly was not the last. It was carried to more places than I could mention. All the family used it of course and even the neighbours came to borrow it if they were going on holiday. So I was very popular for a time.

All good things came to an end as did our holiday, so it was back to the work a day world for me and the return to grumpy Mr Lorimer. Absence hadn't made the heart grow fonder either for him and certainly not for me. Eventually it came to a point when I dreaded going to work in the morning. I knew that things would have to change very soon but how? I couldn't walk out of my job, my mother would never sanction such an action. But things could not continue in the present way.

Suddenly, there appeared a light in the darkness; I heard that the cashier in the grocery store was leaving to get married and that created a vacancy. I was very nervous about applying for this post as the store was a very busy one and carried a lot more responsibility, but there was no alternative; I had to get that job. So once again I applied to the head office for an interview and was granted one to see the Chief Cashier the following week. I was trembling with apprehension and nerves when I duly presented myself at the prescribed time. No mother holding my hand this time. There was the usual test paper and lots of questions which I answered to the best of my ability. They had been in touch with Mr Lorimer to obtain a reference and to my surprise it was a very good one. Either he had a change of heart or he was as glad as I was that we were parting company. There was no question this time of where I had gone to school; the Co-op, unlike some firms, were not interested in what religion their workers favoured, only if you were a good worker and did the job as well as you could. So I got the position and another step up the ladder.

My new boss was a Mr Ross. He was rather small and a bit broad-shouldered, and he suffered from asthma and used to get very breathless from any exertion. I found him to be very strict but fair in my dealings with him. I now had a large cash desk with a small switchboard where I could keep in touch with four of the other Co-op stores in the area. It took me a few days to master the switchboard but I soon became quite expert at using it. There were five other employees in the store: Mr Ross, the second in charge Mr Melville, two younger counter assistants, John Rooney and Danny Docherty, and an older lady Jessie Brown. And now of course myself which made six altogether. My duties were to keep the register up to date. After a transaction had been marked in the customer share book at the counter the book was then passed up to the desk and entered into the ledger. Apart from this I paid out the wages on a Friday morning to the staff.

I can still remember what each individual was paid. Mr Ross got five pounds and three shillings. Mr Melville got three pounds and nine shillings. John Rooney three pounds and four shillings and Danny got two pounds. Jessie Brown got two pounds and six shillings, and last but not least I got the princely sum off 11 shillings and sixpence with the promise of a rise of two shillings on my next birthday. What had I done to deserve this untold wealth? It was a very busy shop and the days passed quickly. There was a lot to do but Ina the Cashier who was leaving had given me a good grounding before she left and I felt that I would be able to cope. The staff were also very helpful which made a great difference to me. Mr Melville was in his late 30s. John Rooney, late 20s, Jessie Brown in her early 40s and Danny Docherty 19 years of age. I did not have much in common with Mr Melville but John, Danny and Jessie became my very good friends after a time. John Rooney was a big bear of a man, tall and well built with fair hair and a smiling face. He was always telling jokes and making us laugh when we were having our tea breaks in the kitchen. Danny was of medium height with straight black hair and the most beautiful big brown eyes with long lashes. Jessie was a spinster who stayed with her mother. She was a kindly soul and very motherly to me. She had worked in the shop for years and although she knew she would never rise any further than her present position she seemed quite happy with her lot in life.

As I mentioned before I had joined the Guide movement a few years previous and we were having a concert in the Co-op hall in a few weeks time. I was singing and acting in a play in the performance and so I brought in a few tickets to sell among the staff. They also purchased one, although I don't suppose it was their idea of great night out. John Rooney had taken one as well but Jessie said he wouldn't likely turn up at the concert, but had just bought the ticket to please me. I was inclined to agree with her but on the night of the concert they all attended the concert, John included, and I was so pleased about that.

The performance went very well and everyone seemed to enjoy it, I had quite a decent singing voice in those days and used to sing all the time, around the house, coming upstairs after work and going downstairs in the morning. All the people used to sing quite a lot in those days and all the men and the boys used to whistle all the time. I don't know the last time I heard anyone whistle. Maybe we didn't have much in the material sense but we seemed to be happier in those days. This was also a happy time in my life. I liked my job, I had my friends and best of all I had my first real boyfriend. As most people would have guessed by now it was Danny. He was a really nice lad and stayed with his mother. His father had died when he was quite young and he had no brothers or sisters, only a few cousins with whom he was quite friendly. He was also a Catholic and unlike most boys of his age a very devout one. We got on really well and after a few weeks he asked me if I would like to go to the theatre with him. I was really keen to do so but I was afraid my mother would not allow it; she thought at 15 years of age I was too young to have a steady boyfriend. I told Danny of my doubts and he had the bright idea of asking Jessie to go with us to act as a chaperone. Nowadays young girls would shriek with laughter, but at that time one had to observe the proper procedure of doing things. Jessie agreed to come with us and my mother was quite happy to see Jessie, Danny and myself going out together. I had a new blue costume and a white blouse and felt like a Princess stepping out with her Prince Charming.

Chapter Four

As I said, this was a happy period in my life. But dark clouds were looming on the horizon. For quite a time there had been worries about events happening in Germany. There had been rumours circulating about the German Jews being treated badly and spat on upon the streets and having their businesses burned down. Adolf Hitler had made no secret of the fact that he wanted rid of non-German people from the country. He wanted to found a master race of pure Aryans only. To this end he had started a group called Hitler Youth and thousands of people were joining their ranks. With all this unrest happening our Prime Minister Neville Chamberlain had gone to Germany the previous year to talk to Hitler and tried to calm things down. He came back to Britain waving a piece of paper and chanting 'peace in our time!' Everyone was very relieved that the danger of war between our two countries had been averted, but not quite convinced that the crisis was really over. There were still rumours that mobilisation of German War weapons was still going on and that Germany was building up a formidable amount of war planes. It turned out that our worst fear would be realised and few months later Hitler's moved into Poland.

Chamberlain sent a letter to Hitler to say that unless he removed his army from Poland by 11am on Sunday 3rd September 1939 then Britain would declare war on Germany. He was to broadcast a message to the people of Britain at that time to tell them of Hitler's decision. I think every family in Britain was gathered round their radios on that day to hear the verdict. I can still remember every word he said. At 11am precisely:

This is London calling, I sent a note to Adolf Hitler to say that unless we heard from him by 11 am today to say that his army would leave Poland immediately then Britain would be at war with Germany. I have to inform you that I have received no such assurance, so Britain is now in a state of war with Germany.

Everyone was in a state of shock and disbelief and so much for that piece of paper. Peace in our time! Only 20 years had passed since the end of the carnage of the 1914-1918 war where hundreds of thousands had died in the mud and filth of Flanders Field and now it was happening all over again. Will man never learn? This was the beginning of the darkest period of our history.

In the previous year when the first rumblings about war had begun we were all issued with gas masks. Even the children had miniature ones, copies of the adults' ones. They were horrible things to wear; they were made of rubber and fitted over your nose and mouth. They emanated a horrible, sickly smell and they came along with a small case and a strap which was slung over your shoulder. We were supposed to carry them at all times in case of a gas attack. Mustard gas had been used in the previous war and many of the soldiers of that time were still suffering from the effects of it 20 years after it had all ended. When we put on the gas masks we looked like creatures from outer space, although appearances were the last things on our minds.

I think of all the things that happened in the next five years - air raids, shortage of food, lack of sleep, and rationing - the worst thing of all was the total blackout. Every house had to cover their windows with black material so that no light showed. There were no street lights and we had to carry a torch everywhere we went, keeping the beam on the ground. The authorities had built baffle walls in front of the building in case of bomb blast, and many a sore head was caused by bumping into these walls in the darkness. Most of the picture halls and theatres were closed, so there was no escape from the grim reality at that time.

It was decided by the higher powers that there should be an evacuation of all school children away from the city to the relative quiet of the country in case of air raids. My younger brother Peter and my young sister were sent to Turriff in Aberdeenshire and my mother was heartbroken. They had never been away from home on their own before and she worried about how they would cope. They were not billeted in the same house, although they were in the same street, so at least they could meet every day and spend time together and that helped a lot.

Food was in very short supply and we were all issued with ration books, so that what little there was would be shared fairly among the people. At that time we were allowed 2oz of butter/margarine and one egg per person per week. In my case I was quite lucky working in a grocery store. When the customers had been given their allowance, any surplus was divided among the staff by Mr Ross. This was a great help to my mother as she only could take butter and couldn't take her tea without sugar. So I usually managed to get these commodities to help out.

My romance was not going so well at this time. Danny had left the store to work in an aircraft factory, much better wages and he was on shift work and did a lot of overtime, so I did not see a lot of him, usually about once a week. It was the same for everyone at that time.

It had taken a war to bring prosperity. Business was booming and wages were high but there was not very much to spend it on. Even furniture was in short supply and only utility articles were made, functional but nothing fancy or ornate, and there was a six month waiting list for delivery. We very seldom saw any fruit in

25

the shop as it was kept mostly for the children who had green ration books and these had to be shown before you could purchase the fruit. Most children had never seen a banana till the war was over as these came from abroad and the shipping lines were dangerous due to the presence of German U-Boats.

Conscription had now started and queues of young men were lining up to enlist for the Armed Forces. Both of my brothers were in reserved occupations and did not require to enlist, but my brother Joe joined the Merchant Navy and John went into the Civilian Home Guard. Joe was a 3rd Officer in the SS Vimera and was doing convoy work on the Russian Murmansk run. He looked very handsome in his officer's uniform and my mother was very proud of him as we all were. But also a bit afraid for him too as it was a dangerous job he was doing.

Some of the children who had been evacuated were starting to drift back home, as so far we had been spared any air attacks, although London was not so fortunate. My young brother and sister had returned. Chrissie was brought back by my parents, but Peter with a friend had already hitch hiked home before her.

Rationing was getting worse and even water had to be used sparingly; we were told to use only five inches of water in the bath which was hardly enough to keep your feet clean.

At least the cinemas had opened up again but there was no light relief in a visit there either. The news reels were full of the terrible disasters that were happening in London; the city was being bombed mercilessly almost every night and the people were spending most nights in the underground air raid shelters and going to work next morning with very little or no sleep.

On May 1940 our Armies were fighting in France, trying to stem the progress of the Germans who were marching on Paris. After a heavy battle our troops were surrounded and stranded on the beach at Dunkirk with no means of escape. When news of what was happening got back to Britain, Churchill broadcast a message to the British people informing them of the plight of our troops and asking for anyone who owned a boat to try to get to their aid. Within a few days an army of boats of all sizes and description were sailing across the channel to the rescue. Some were small and could only hold one or two passengers, others were large and could take ten or twelve but all of them were determined to help in any way they could. One could only guess what emotions were felt by these weary and embattled men when they saw this flotilla of ships coming towards them. The boats came as near to the beach as possible and the Germans were kept back with the gunfire from those who were able to fight back and who had ammunition. Some were wounded and had to be carried out to safety by the ones who were able to help them. Others walked unaided to the boats and the rescue began. After a few days thousands had been rescued in this way. Of course they could not rescue everyone and thousands were left; the wounded and the unfit were left at the mercy of the enemy. A minor miracle had been achieved and the people of Britain rejoiced.

It was not until after the war was over and the prisoners of war returned that we found out what had happened to the few survivors of that battle. They had been captured as prisoners of war and force-marched for days to camps miles away. The sick and the wounded were dropping like flies due to weakness and malnutrition and those who collapsed were shot were they lay. Such is man's inhumanity to man. I visited a Dunkirk a few years later after the war and found it a small, dull town with a few shops scattered around which I presumed to be a market square. There was nothing there to remind one of the small miracle that had occurred on the beaches or its brutal and bloody aftermath.

In that same month of that year the much wanted and supposed impregnable line of fortifications knows as the Maginot Line had been breached by the Germans. This was a line of fortifications dividing France from Germany. It had been built before the war on the instructions of the then War Minister, Andre Maginot. The defences were never really tested on this occasion as the Germans simply bypassed then and went through Belgium instead on their way to France. Paris was occupied soon after and France fell to the German Army.

As I said we had been fortunate so far and we had no air raids in Glasgow but all that changed in March 1941 when dozens of planes came over with the Clyde shipyard as a target. All night long the bombardment went on while we sat in our air raid shelter and prayed for our lives to be saved. When the all-clear siren sounded after dawn we emerged from the shelter and were shocked by what we saw. There was dust, debris and fires as far as you could see. Buildings with half their roof ripped off and people running around dazed and speechless with grief and fear. Nothing could have prepared us for this amount of destruction and to think that the people had been suffering this nightly for months. How could this small island of ours stand up to the might of Germany and their allies with the resources we had?

Our shipping fleet was small and we were losing more ships everyday to the German U-Boats, our Air Force was in its infancy and short of trained pilots, and our Armies were deployed in so many fronts and losing hundreds of young lives every day. In spite of all this there was still something of the British bulldog spirit in all of us and the belief that if the Londoners could suffer this and still carry on then so could we.

As someone said, 'Cometh the hour, cometh the man!' and we had the man, our Prime Minister Winston Churchill. He was a chubby man with the face of a bull dog and a cigar always stuck in his mouth. Not a very romantic figure but with a great gift or oratory that raised our spirits in the darkest days to come. His speech at the height of the Battle of Britain when our air force took on the might of the German Air Force will never be forgotten. *Never in the fields of human conflict has so much been owed to so many by so few.* And another when people's spirits were at their lowest: *we will fight them in the hills, we will fight them on the streets, we will fight them on the beaches, but we will never surrender.*

As I said we were on our own for the first few years of the war but in December 1941 America was suddenly forced into the front line when the Japanese attacked Pearl Harbour. The Japanese Prime Minister was actually in America at that time taking part in peace talks with President Roosevelt when it happened. Suddenly a string of planes appeared out of the blue, strafing the planes on the ground with gun fire and sinking the ships in the harbour. The raid was of comparatively short duration but the destruction was immense. Suddenly the great and powerful United States of America was our ally and we no longer stood alone. In a comparatively short time the Yanks as they came to be known started arriving in our midst to a very mixed reception. Some people thought that we should be grateful to them because they would now be standing side by side with us and sharing the load. Others were more sceptical saying that they had only came into the war after being attacked themselves. They had stayed neutral for the first two years of the war and unlike us they had not had to suffer air raids, food shortage or any kind of depravation.

In some quarters they were welcomed with open arms. The American troops had access to all the luxury items that had been denied to us for years: silk stockings, nylons, chocolates and all kinds of tinned food and fruit. So the young girls flocked to them in droves and the young men had a saying about them: *Overpaid, over-sexed and over here*! This was due to jealousy of course, but who could blame them? When there was any entertainment going on at the American base they would lay on a bus to take the girls there and it was always full to capacity.

Meanwhile the raids continued and now it was with bigger and more lethal bombs and even land mines. One of these landed in Maryhill, a short distance from our store and one of our shop assistants Rita was buried for a night and a day before being dug out of the debris. She was in the hospital for weeks with shrapnel wounds to her head and had to have plastic surgery.

There were quite a few changes happening in the shop also. The men had left and gone into the factories and only Jessie remained of the original staff. A married couple had taken the place of Danny and John Rooney. This was contrary to the policy of the Co-op as no married couple had ever worked in the same store before. But with so many men in the forces, the change in policy was inevitable.

Mr. Ross of course was still in charge as he was too old for the forces and with his asthmatic condition was unfit for military service in any case. He has started smoking some substance that was supposed to help his asthma. it was not menthol as that was a pleasant aromatic odour, but the kind that he smoked left a sickly sweet and unpleasant smell in the air. We used to steer clear of the kitchen where he had his smoke after his cup of tea. There were no anti-smoking laws in those days and the people lit up whenever they wished to do so.

My romance was still going on but were not seeing one another as often as before due to his long working hours and the regular shifts. My younger brother Peter was now 14 years of age and had started working as a page boy in one of the big picture houses in town. He was allowed a free pass every week which admitted two people to get free admission to the show. On one occasion he had given me one of the passes so that Danny and I could see the film, I don't think my mother was very happy about our relationship but as I was now 16 years of age she allowed me to go, but not before giving me a lecture about what nice girls should and should not allow and assurance that I would be home no later than ten o'clock. Of course she did not know Danny very well as she had only met him once when we had gone to the theatre with Jessie. So I knew she would be grilling Peter when he returned. Peter told me later that when she questioned him about what Danny looked like he said that he was okay but had these big brown eyes and as he succinctly put it, 'Like a cow looking over a dyke'. So much for my black haired Adonis, reduced to a figure of fun by the brutal honesty of my 14 year old brother.

My older brother Joe was now courting a girl he had known for years and was planning to get married on his next leave. Betty was a nice girl and we all liked her. Joe had had lots of girlfriends as he was a very handsome fellow but now had decided to settle down. The wedding reception was held in the Co-op hall after a church service of course and as Betty was a Catholic too there was no problem at all. It was a really good night and my father was in charge of the bar, so nobody was allowed to get too merry and become a nuisance to other people. Betty of course was dressed in white and Joe was married in his uniform. Betty had her friend Pat as Bridesmaid and Joe had one of his fellow officers as his best man. It was a very happy occasion and we all had a jolly evening. Betty's mother had died when Betty was in her teens, so she gave a bouquet of flowers to my mother in her place.

By this time the war was opening up on many fronts. Marshall Montgomery was in charge of the 8th Army in the Middle East known as the Desert Rats and his adversary was Field Marshall Rommel, a very distinguished General revered by his men and even admired by our troops for his leadership and his expertise in desert warfare. In the Far East the Japanese were advancing steadily on the road to Singapore while the Germans were on their way to Paris. By this time the Australians and the Canadians had also came into the war. So, there was fighting in most parts of the world. There seemed to be no end in sight and people were getting dispirited and longed desperately for some respite. There were rumours about Jews in Germany being herded into labour camps but nobody seemed to know if this was true or otherwise.

We were still suffering heavy losses in ships and planes although very steadily the Air Force was gaining strength and more pilots were being trained than ever before.

On the Home Front rationing was dreadful. If you saw a queue outside a shop you joined in the hope of getting something that you hope could make your rations go a little further. There were shortages of everything; no paper bags, no pins or needles or thread. All these little things you took for granted were now luxuries. My mother had a white cotton shopping bag which she scrubbed daily and when she went shopping everything was put and carried in the same bag. Bread, vegetables, and everything else was put in together and sorted out when you got home. As I said there were no bags, no wrapping paper, nothing to put your purchases in.

The girls and the women used to use lard instead of face cream and lipsticks were a luxury you hoarded using it to the last drop because you did not know when you would get another one. There were no hair grips and the women used to tie a thin scarf around their head and tuck the hair round it to keep it tidy.

There was no television those days but most households had a radio and we all used to listen to the news in the evening. A renegade Englishman who defected to Germany a few years previously now broadcast a message from Germany every evening, gloating about our losses of ships and planes and how well the Germans were doing in the war. We named him Lord Haw Haw as he had a very posh voice and was rumoured to be one of the gentry in our country. Of course most of what he said was German propaganda but we listened anyway, hoping to get some information about what was happening.

Our next-door neighbour Mrs. Robinson had three daughters and one of the girls Mary was the same age as I was and quite soon we became good friends. She caught a bad cold and a rasping cough and her mother decided to call in the doctor to see if she could get a bottle to help her cough but to her horror she was told that Mary had tuberculosis. This disease was quite prevalent in Glasgow at that time and there was a bit of a stigma attached to it. It was believed to have been caused by bad housing and a poor diet. The patient was usually sent to a sanatorium where they lay in bed on a veranda as it was believed that the fresh air, rest and nourishing food was the only cure. In this case the disease had been diagnosed too late and had too strong a hold and Mary died a few months later, aged 16. Less than two years later the oldest girl Sarah died at 21 with the same disease. Life can be cruel.

My father had a small black moustache which he was very proud of and always kept neatly trimmed and was most annoyed when he discovered that Adolf Hitler had one that was almost identical to his. He came home from work and told my mother that some children had shouted 'Adolf' at him when he passed by and he was not amused. He was now working a 12-hour day and was beginning to look very tired and worn. My mother worried a lot about him and had also the added anxiety about my brother Joe who was still on the Murmansk run taking much needed supplied to Russia. This was a very dangerous voyage with the threat of the U-Boats being so prevalent.

My mother and I were listening to the morning news as we normally did before I went to work, my mother suddenly let out a scream and when I ran into the lounge she was crying bitterly. The news reader was talking about a convoy that had been attacked by the German U-Boats and were surrounded by them. He then gave a list of the ships that were involved and one of these was the SS Vimera, my brother's ship. I did not get to work that morning as I couldn't leave my mother is such a state of grief. It was three fear-filled days before we heard that the Vimera had escaped and had managed to sail into safer water. My brother told us later that every man on the ship was on their knees praying for a safe delivery and by the grace of God they survived to fight another day. I think my parents aged ten years in those three days before they knew my brother was safe and well.

My family circle was getting smaller now that my eldest sister Annie and my brother Joe were now married and living in their own homes. Annie had married an ex-regular soldier who had served in India in the 1914-18 War. He was ten years older than my sister, and my mother was very much against the match at the start; not only because of the age gap but because regular soldiers did not have a good reputation at that time. They were regarded as rough types and too fond of drinking and getting into trouble. Not the kind who

34

made good husband material. As it happens Jimmy was not like that at all, but it took a long time for my mother to accept him as part of the family. He worked in Blochairn steel works on shift work and a few months after they were married when he was on nightshift a loud knocking of the door woke my sister. When she went to answer it found Jimmy standing swaying on the doorstep with glazed eyes and muttering incoherently. With my mother's foreboding about drunken soldiers going through her mind she dragged him into the lobby, pushed him into the bedroom and locked the door from the outside and went to bed seething with anger.

The next morning one of his work mates came to enquire about Jimmy's state of health and received a tongue lashing from my sister about letting Jimmy getting into such a drunken state. When the man got a chance to speak he told my sister that there had been a small gas explosion at the works the previous night and some of the men had been affected by the gas. He had offered to take Jimmy home but he was adamant he would manage on his own. When he had started walking home the gas started to have an effect which caused the dazed state of his appearance. Poor Jimmy. He learned that night who was wearing the trousers in his house. He had joined the army at 16 years of age because of a very unhappy home life with a bullying father and a mother who was too afraid of her husband to do anything about it. He had spent several years in India and while he was there he had a beautiful tattoo of the crucifixion drawn on his back. It was a wonderful work of art even down to the life like nails on the hands and feet of Christ. He had a lovely deep voice and sang in the works choir. His party piece was 'Grannie's Highland Hame!' Every time I hear of it I think of Jimmy who in the years that followed was like another big brother to us all. My sister Annie had a very forceful personality and as she was the oldest of the siblings was inclined to boss the rest of us.

She was a machinist and collar maker in the Tootal factory, and she had risen to the rank of supervisor in her job. When she married, my mother had spoken to our landlord, or factor as we called them, and managed to get her a flat in our building so she was never very far away from the family. We used to have dinner at her house quite often and one Sunday after we had our meal she asked us if we wanted dessert which was jelly and fruit. Of course we were delighted to accept the offer. She pressed us to finish the jelly which was in a large bowl and we appreciated her generosity but what she omitted to tell us was that morning she had been cutting Jimmy's hair and had accidentally dropped the clippers into the bowl. We did not notice anything and scoffed the lot but it could have been a hairy experience.

Chapter Five

My romance was now over. We had a stupid row over something trivial, he called me childish and I stalked off in a huff. For over a week he bombarded me with phone calls and letters of apology, but I was too proud to give in and eventually the calls stopped. It had always rankled with Danny that I was 4 years younger than he was and had often said that he had felt that he was a cradle snatcher and vowed he would not tell his mother about our relationship until I was at least 17 years of age when he would be 21 and considered old enough to be in a permanent attachment. The irony of this was that I was just a few months from my 17th birthday and now it had all gone wrong. They say that you never forget your first love and I think this is true as even now years later I still have fond memories of him and what might have been.

Oddly enough about two years later one of our customers said to me, 'You would not guess who I was talking to last night in town.' When I asked who it was she said, 'It was Danny who used to work in the shop and he was asking if you still worked there and were you still single?' She said that I still worked there but I was courting, so he told her to give me his regards. So it seemed he had not quite forgotten me after all.

My sister-in-law, Betty who had an aunt who lived in Kilmun, a little village near Dunoon which was very popular sea side resort. She was intending to visit her one weekend and asked me if I would like to go with her. She warned me that it was very quiet place and that I would find it a bit boring, but as I had nothing else planned I agreed to go with her. Her aunt stayed in a little house above the harbour wall and that night when I lay in bed I could hear the water lapping up against the wall. It was such a soothing sound and such a peaceful feeling as I lay there and listened to it that I soon dropped off and knew nothing more until the sun shining through the window and woke me up.

Betty and I had a lot of time chat that weekend and she told me a bit about herself. I knew that her mother had died when she was quite young but not much else about her past history. She had two older brothers and after her mother had died her father had decided to emigrate to America with the two boys, leaving Betty to stay with his sister Susan until they got settled and he was able to send for her and her younger brother Danny to join them in America. Her aunt Susan was a spinster and was able to look after the children until they could join their father.

It took a few years until they were established in a decent home and had steady jobs and he was able to send for them. By this time the children were settled in Glasgow and were quite happy and moreover Aunt Susan did not want them to go away. So it was decided to leave things as they were. Of course they kept in touch regularly by letter but as far as I know Betty did not see her father again.

The war was still dragging on and the air raids continued, although they were more sporadic and less severe that hitherto. The shipyards in Clydebank had been decimated and hardly a house left undamaged in the area. So I suppose that had been the main reason that Glasgow had been targeted in the first place. We did not always go to the shelter now when a siren sounded although the shelter was not as miserable and cold a place as it had been. We had a few benches to sit on and a small prima stove to heat the place, and there was even a rug on the floor. I say a rug but it was really an old moth-eaten fur coat that someone had unearthed from the wardrobe. It kept our feet warm and off the stone floor. Most nights now when the sirens sounded we all gathered in a neighbour's house on the ground floor of the building. We had a big flask filled with hot tea and sometimes a few sandwiches or a packet of biscuits to keep us going. I suppose it was not the safest place to go as if the bombs had dropped on the building and it had collapsed we would all have been buried in the debris, but it made us feel happier than we felt in the shelter.

My mother had a big handbag in which she kept all her insurance policies and this was the first thing she would grab as soon as the sirens went. We used to laugh at her but she said she felt better knowing she had them with her, although what good they would have been to us if we had all been blown up, I don't really know. Still if it made her happy that was all that mattered to us.

London was still being bombed nightly and even Buckingham Palace had taken a hit. The damage was not very extensive but when Queen Elizabeth and King George were on a visit to London to view the bomb damage the Queen said At least now she could now look the Eastenders in the face.

I have heard it said that human beings come into two categories: morning people and night people. The morning people are up early and ready to face the day ahead; the night people only really come to life in the darker hours. If this is the case then my family were equally divided. Annie, John and Chrissie were morning people. Peter, Joe and myself were night owls.

My brother John was always a bit of a loner. He did not have many friends and seemed to prefer his own company. He would spend hours making things with his meccano set and models of ships or planes with his airfix. He did not do very well at school and only excelled at woodwork lessons or joinery class (shades of my father). When he was 16 years old and the right age for an apprenticeship he wanted to study engineering, but as there was not a vacancy in that trade at the time he had gone in for brass moulding instead. He was not a bit interested in his appearance and my mother was always telling him off about now washing his neck or combing his hair but no matter what she said John never changed his ways. He seemed to enjoy being a bit of a slob.

Peter on the other hand was very fastidious and took care of his appearance. He was quite small but very neat and tidy. It was difficult to believe that two brothers could be so unlike one another.

One Saturday night about midnight Peter was sitting in the lounge reading a book when he heard a key going into the front door and someone trying to open it. Everyone was in bed asleep, so he knew it must be a stranger. He went into the hall, pulled open the door and was confronted by a strange man trying to open the door. He pulled him into the hall and shouted to my father to come and help him. My father still dazed and half asleep, jumped out of the bed and ran into the hall. He saw Peter and a stranger struggling on the floor. The scullery door was open and there was an empty lemonade bottle laying on the table, so my father lifted it and hit the intruder on the head, which stunned him momentarily. By this time all the family were awake and standing in the hall asking what was happening and looking at the stranger who was now conscious and laying on the floor. When Peter told them what had happened, my mother was in a panic and was sure that my father would be put in jail for assault. Meanwhile the intruder had got out of the opened door and disappeared downstairs. It was a long time after before we got to bed and we were fearful of what was going to happen to my father if the police got involved, which of course was sure to happen. The next morning two policemen came to our door to question my father about what had happened the previous night and he told them how and why he had acted in the way he had done, thinking that a burglar had tried to break into our house and was attacking Peter. As it turned out there was a simple explanation as to why the intruder had been trying to gain access to the house; he was soldier home on leave and his parents had just moved into the building next to us a few weeks previously. Coming home in the blackout he had mistaken the entry and had come into our block of flats by mistake. His parents had given him a key but of course it did not fit our lock so he had been fumbling with his key and trying to open the door when Peter heard him. With him being away in the army we had not seen him before, so he was a total stranger to us. The police gave my father a warning but because of his age (he was almost 60) and the circumstances and also the fact the young man had not been seriously harmed they decided not to take any further action, which was a great relief to us all and especially to my mother.

Although both of my parents were from Irish descent, all the family had been born in Glasgow and considered themselves Scottish. But not so John who was into everything Irish and very proud of his roots.

We had a radiogram which my father used to play in the evenings and lots of records mainly of Irish songs and sung by Irish singers. John knew most of them by heart and was always singing them. There was a variety show from Radio Éireann to which we all listened. At the end of it they would always finish off with 'The Soldiers' Song' which was the unofficial Irish Anthem at that time. When it was played, John used to stand to attention and salute and we all used to laugh at him and say how stupid he looked. Children can be cruel to anyone who is different from them and John was definitely different to the rest of us.

I looked up to Joe and admired him but he was so much older than me there was no common ground between us. My sister Annie was in the same category and Chrissie to me was still the baby of the family, so I guess at the time Peter, who was closest to me in age, was my favourite brother, with us being alike in lots of ways. In later years my sisters and I became much closer.

My mother had managed to acquire a length of gents' suiting from a friend who worked in a clothing mill and thought it would make me a nice costume. There was a lady who lived up the street who was a dressmaker and she agreed to make the suit. The cloth was of a nice shade of brown with a thin line of silver running through it. After a few weeks and quite a few fittings the suit was ready to wear. My mother had bought me a new pink blouse with a new pair of shoes in the same colour but with a slighter higher heel than I usually wore. When I tried on my new outfit I could not believe the difference it made as I looked quite elegant and grown up. The jacket was slim fitting and the skirt had four box pleats. For the first time in my life I felt really pretty. Of course I only wore it for best and only on Sundays. At that time most people got dressed on Sundays and the women and girls always wore a hat when they were going out. Clothes were now on the ration and we were issued with a book of clothing tokens to buy them. Even a pair of stockings cost two tokens and these were ugly thick lisle ones and anything but flattering to your legs. To overcome this, the girls used to buy a bottle of suntan lotion to put on their legs and some of them were using an eyebrow pencil to draw a line up the centre to look like a seam in the stocking. I tried this once or twice but did not make a very good job of it. So I decided just to use the tan on its own.

My sister-in-law Betty had an aunt and an uncle who stayed in Hamilton, a few miles outside Glasgow whom she used to visit on a Sunday. The husband Mr Blake owned two public houses in that area and Sunday was the only day the family were at home as at that time there was no public houses open on a Sunday. The only place you could buy a drink was at a hotel and only then if you were having a meal as well.

Betty asked John and I if we would like to come with her as the Blakes had a son and daughter about our age and she thought that they would be company for us to talk to and that we could get to know each other. Of course I wore my new outfit and my mother made sure that John was well scrubbed before we left.

The Blakes stayed in a nice house on the outskirts of the town and when we arrived we were shown into the lounge which was very well furnished and immaculately clean. Betty introduced us to Mr Blake who shook hands with us and welcomed us into his home, and then introduced us to his son and daughter. His wife merely nodded to us in acknowledgement but his son and daughter smiled and shook hands. They had laid on a nice meal for us but I did not feel comfortable as I could fell Mrs Blakes eyes on me all the time as if she was appraising me and taking notes of all I did. I was glad when the meal was over and we moved into the sitting room. The daughter was very quiet but the son Jack chatted away to me asking me about my work and what I enjoyed doing in my spare time. He told me he played football for the works' team and he was working in an engineering factory. All the time we were chatting I could feel his mother's eyes on me and was very glad when after tea Mr Blake said he would run us home in the car. Betty and John seemed quite pleased by the way things had gone, but I felt that I had never spent such a miserable afternoon in my life. Just as I was leaving Mrs Blake said to me, 'I see that you are using that tan on your legs. I am afraid my daughter has not got such modern ideas.' In other words, 'You are a common hussy and we don't want to know you.' I didn't think I would be invited back there again.

Jack had come in the car with us but we did not talk much on the way home. To my amazement I received a letter from him in a few days, asking me if I would like to go to a show with him. I wasn't attracted to him in a romantic way but he seemed a nice lad and as he had given me a phone number in his letter I decided to call him and say that I would like to go with him. We had a nice evening and he was very attentive and easy to talk to, so when he asked me to go with him to see a film the following week I agreed. He loved his football and told me they were in the final of his league and were hoping to win it. We went out on a few dates after that but he always got me home quite early as he had a bus to catch to get back to Hamilton. On one of our outings he gave me a little chain bracelet that he had made at work and attached to it was the medal that all the football team had received when they won the final match of the league. I was quite touched with this and agreed to take good care of it.

On one of our outings the film had finished later than expected so he missed his last bus home and had to walk which took him about an hour to get there. When I next met him he told that when he got home the door was locked against him and he had to sleep in the garage.

There was a variety show coming to the theatre which we both wished to see but the tickets were very expensive and I told him not to spend all his money on me. However he was adamant that he could afford it. So we agreed a time and a place to meet. When the time came I arrived at our meeting place in plenty of time but after waiting for almost a half hour there was no sign of Jack. I thought something must have prevented him from coming so I just went down to my friend's house and we both went to the pictures instead. When I got home I was amazed to find Mr and Mrs Blake sitting in our lounge with my mother and father. As soon as I appeared my mother said, 'Where have you been?' and when I said I had been to the pictures with my friend Nora she asked me if I had seen Jack Blake. I could not understand what was going on and why she was questioning me or why Mr and Mrs Blake were there. It appeared that Jack had been missing for three days and they wondered if I knew where he had gone. I was as mystified as they were, and I explained that I had been supposed to meet him that night but he had not appeared, and that I had not seen him since the previous week. My mother knew that I was telling the truth and said so to Mr and Mrs Blake and eventually they left. When they had gone my mother made me promise that I would not see Jack Blake again and I agreed that I did not want to be in the centre of a family feud. I heard from my sister-in-law later what had happened. It seemed that Mrs Blake had been going through the drawers in Jack's bedroom and had found the theatre tickets. When he said that they were for him and I she had forbidden him to go and tore the tickets up in front of him. Jack had stormed out and said he was leaving for good and had then gone missing. I believe he came back a few days later but I never got in touch again to find out what had really happened. He had told me that the reason he had given me a phone number was because his mother used to read his mail and after what had happened I am sure he was right. I don't know if it was only me that she disliked or if any other girl he was fond of would have suffered the same fate. I was very sorry for Jack for having a mother like her but was I was glad to be out of it all. As it happened a few weeks later the bracelet snapped and I lost the chain and medal.

Chapter Six

I was now passed my 17th birthday footloose and fancy free and becoming a bit bored with the sameness of my everyday life. Lots of girls of my age had started joining the armed forces and I toyed with the idea of doing the same but to what service was I most suited? I did not fancy the ATS with all the square bashing. The Women's Naval Service - the WRENS they were called - had a very smart uniform which I very much admired but with my history of sea sickness I had to admit that a life on the ocean wave was not for me. So that left only the Land Army. I could quite see myself working in the beautiful green countryside and breathing the fresh country air, but as my mother pointed out to me I would have to be up at dawn, summer and winter, in order to feed the animals or milk the cows. This aspect of the job did not sound very appealing and anyhow what did I know about looking after animals? Living in Glasgow the only animals I was familiar with wer cats, dogs and an occasional horse. Taking all these factors into account I decided that I would be better sticking to what I knew best and staying where I was until something better turned up.

Before the war had started very few of the girls or women smoked cigarettes. The men in my family very rarely did, or at least never in the house, although my father had always smoked a clay pipe or a cigar on special occasions. But that was all changing now as more of the women were working in factories and taking up the habit. I had always thought it was a horrible, filthy habit and I thought that the girls who smoked looked common and unfeminine, but as time went by even I got used to the idea and realised that this practice was here to stay. There were hoardings and advertisements all over the town and even on the tram cars advertising all the different brands of cigarettes. One depicted a young handsome man standing on the corner of the street with a cigarette between his fingers and a caption underneath which read, 'You're never alone with a Strand.' A new brand of cigarette. With all this propaganda being thrown at us, my friend Nora and I decided we would have a go. So between us we bought a packet of 10 cigarettes but as we dared not smoke in the house with our parents present we had to wait for the times when we were on our own and out together to experiment. The first time we lit up we felt a bit sick and dizzy but we soldiered on and soon that feeling passed and we began to enjoy the sensation. A few weeks later I was at home as it was half day closing at the shop. My mother went down to the back yard to beat the carpets and as I knew she would be gone for a while I decided I would have a quick cigarette. I went into the bathroom, locked the door and lit up. I opened the window to let the smoke out so that my mother would not smell it when she came back home. But a few minutes later I heard the front door opening and I heard my mother shouting, 'Something is burning!'. She had looked up and saw the smoke coming out of the window and thought the worst had happened. Of course I had to admit that I had been smoking and she was really angry and said that my father would be really disappointed in me if her ever found out. I lived in dread for the next few days waiting for the explosion to erupt but nothing happened. So I knew my mother had not said anything to him.

A few weeks later my father was doing some woodwork and got a splinter in his finger and I asked me if I had a pair of tweezers so that he could take it out. I told him there was a pair in my handbag and told him to use them. When he went to open my bag I suddenly remembered too late that I had a packet of cigarettes in there as well. I waited for the explosion but all he said was, 'I see you are at this game as well.' I suppose he must have seen other women smoking at work and was not as shocked as my mother had been when she discovered my secret vice. Although the secret was out I still did not dare smoke in the home until months later. I had got off lightly this time but I was not going to push my luck.

It was now 1942 and the war was still dragging on, although we were now beginning to hold our own in the air battles and were shooting down more planes than ever before. We had a name for the pilots of the Air Force and called them the Brylcream Boys as they were mostly young and handsome and looked very dashing in their smart blue uniform and their fur-lined flying jackets.

In North Africa the 8th Army The Desert Rats were fighting a decisive battle at El Alamain and Rommel's Army were in retreat. In London however, the bombing went on and now a new missile had been added to the arsenal of destruction. It was a flying bomb called the Doodle Bug and was causing massive damage in the capital. Rationing was still very bad but a couple of items had been added to our larder which helped to eke out our food allowance: powdered egg and powdered potato. When liquid was added to these items they tasted almost as good as the real thing. The housewives had also discovered mashed carrot was a good substitute for sugar when it was used to bake scones or cakes. Necessity is definitely the mother of invention.

Unlike food, cigarettes had never been rationed but when the shopkeepers received their order they were usually put under the counter and only given to their regular customers. When stocks became low some of the smaller shops would split the packets and sell them loose in two's or three's for a few coppers and usually with a match provided. Even then it was not always the same brand of cigarettes that you received. Perhaps one or two of the popular names and a few of the less popular brands. One of the latter was a cigarette called Pasha. It was made in Turkey and smelled of burnt carpet. When anyone lit one of these the people nearby had to hold their noses as the smell was so disgusting. As I mentioned before, if you saw a queue outside a shop you joined it in the hope of getting something to add to your rations. I of course I could not do this as I was at work all day but my mother could and although she disliked the thought of me smoking quite a few times she would slip me a packet of cigarettes that she had queued up to get for me. Such is a mother's love: hate the sin but love the sinner. On that hoarding which advertised *you are never alone with a Strand* it should have also stated *you will always be left alone with a Pasha*.

In August of that year Rommel's Army was defeated by the 8th Army led by General Montgomery who was later knighted for the achievement of this victory. There were still strong rumours about the fate of the Jewish people in Germany. It was said that they had been segregated from the German people and forced into small communes with other Jews, and also that professional people among them such as lawyers and doctors had been banned from practising their profession and were pressured into taking menial jobs in order to survive. It was also said that they had to wear clothes with the badge of Star of David on them so that everyone would know their nationality. At home the tide of war was slowly turning our way and there was even talk of opening up a second front, although this information was very hush-hush and we did not know if it was true or not.

My sister Annie now had a young family and Jimmy her husband had booked a holiday for them in Salcoats, a small holiday resort on the River Clyde. My mother said I should go with her to help her with the children as Jimmy could not get the time off work and would only be going at the weekends. She said also that it would be a holiday for me. I was not very thrilled at the prospect but agreed to go. As I said before, my sister Annie was a very forceful character and was inclined to be a bit bossy. The first few days of our holiday went quite smoothly and I thought maybe it would work out alright. By the following week I was beginning to regret my decision to accompany her. As I said previously she was a morning person and was at her best in the early hours, but I wasn't and when she woke me at 7am to go for the breakfast rolls I was not very pleased to say the least. After the second or third morning of this happening I said I was not going again and Danny was furious. I did not mind helping out but I was not getting up at the crack of dawn in order for her to get hot rolls for breakfast. She wrote to my mother complaining about my behaviour, I was sent home in disgrace and Chrissie was sent down to replace me. All I said to her was, 'Good luck, but don't expect to have any long, lazy mornings in bed'.

At work we had a new member of the staff, a young man from Inverness who was staying for a few months with his sister in Glasgow. He was tall and quite handsome, with blue eyes and fair wavy hair. He did not have any friends locally so we had a few outings together. It suited both of us as he was looking for company and I was quite pleased to have such an attractive escort. His name was George McKenzie and he had a lovely speaking voice, very soft but with a lilt in it, so unlike the broad vowels of the Glaswegians. They say that the people of Dublin and Inverness speak the purest English and after knowing George I quite agree with it. Our liaison did not last very long, only a few months as he began to feel homesick and was missing his family

50

and he decided to return to Inverness. We parted on good terms and I was sorry to see him go as he had been very good company for me and was a really nice person.

At this time ballroom dancing was a passion in Glasgow and all the dance halls were always packed to capacity and it was said that the best dancers in the world came from our city. So if you did not dance you were definitely not part of the social scene.

I had been to a few social nights which included dancing at our local church all and learned the basic steps, but in no sense would I ever consider myself proficient in the art. My brother Joe and his wife Betty were good dancers and had first learned at a small dancing club called *Diamonds Academy of Dance* and this was still going strong. They had advised me to go there if I wanted to learn the proper steps as they gave tuition lessons before each dance and then you could put into practice what you had learned. I thought this was good advice and decided to try it out. So I enrolled at *Diamonds* and turned up for my first session. The hall was not very large but there was quite a good attendance. When the dance was announced the MC and his partner gave a demonstration and invited the learners to have a go. The boys were out on one side of the dance floor, with the girls on the other side facing each other. This gave us the chance to appraise one another and for the boys to pick out the prettiest girls that they wanted as partners. When the music started the boys made a mad dash across the floor and picked their favourite girl to dance with. The girls nervously hoping they would be one of the lucky ones and not left standing like a wall flower. The first dance was a waltz and I had learned the rudiments of this dance before so when I was picked to dance I managed to get round the floor without making a show of myself. The quick step followed and I was lucky enough to have a partner who was more experienced than I was. So I found it quite easy to follow his guidance. I was starting to get quite confident now and enjoying myself. The next demonstration was for a tango. It was a very different kind of dance from the previous ones; you were held much closer by your partner and there were a lot of intricate moves and turns. But my partner had said it was his favourite dance so I knew he must be quite expert at it. I managed to follow him for a few minutes but when he turned me round quite unexpectedly the heel of my shoe caught in the turn-up of his trousers and we landed in an untidy heap on the floor. We looked so ridiculous laying there that I broke into a fit of nervous giggles, but he was not amused. He glared at me, dusted himself down and stomped off the floor in high dudgeon. It was only his pride that had been hurt, but that was enough for him and I did not see him again for the rest of the evening. I continued going for lessons and did become quite a good dancer eventually, so the lessons had been worth it. The Yanks had brought in a few dances of their own, mainly the jitterbug and the jive, but I never really mastered them. As they say, you can't win them all.

As I have mentioned before, both of my parents were of Irish descent. Lots of their friends were of the same origin and as my father was quite a raconteur he was always in great demand for wakes and subsequent funerals of his friends. The wake was strictly an Irish tradition when the male friends of the deceased got together to give the departed one a good send off with songs and jokes and memories of their life. This was to help speed them on their way to heaven, or its alternative. For the funerals my father had two bowler hats, one with a white satin lining and the other one with orange and these were used alternately. With a white shirt, regulation black tie and suit my father was ready for any emergency. During the week he always wore his dungarees and his cloth cap but at the weekend it was his suit, shirt and tie and trilby hat. My mother had told me that he had always been very clothes-conscious when he was young and when they were courting he wore the latest fashion of that time: black suit, white shirt with a high starched collar and with the cuffs overshooting his wrists by a couple of inches, a forerunner of the Teddy Boys perhaps. My parents were married in 1910 when they were both 25 years of age.

There was a family called Davey who stayed in our street. Mrs Davey was a rather plump, faded blonde with three of a family, Jack, Harry and Ellen. Jack was the oldest of the brood. Harry a few years younger and Ellen the baby of the family. It seemed that Mr. Davey had died a few years previously, before they moved into our area, when he was only in his early 40's. Mrs Davey loved having young people around and their house was always full of their childrens' friends and was more or less an open house, especially at the weekend when there was always a cup of tea ready for anyone who stopped in for a visit or a chat. I went there a few times, usually on Sunday afternoon as there was not much else to do at that time except to go for walks or visit friends and families.

On one of these visits Harry told me that one of the ships he had been working on was due to be launched in a few weeks time and asked me if I would like to go with him to see this event. It seems that there was an open invitation to any worker who had worked on the ship and they could bring their wives or girlfriends as well. I had never seen a ship being launched before so I jumped at the chance as this would be a new experience for me. When the great day arrived we all gathered at the shipyard, dressed in our best clothes and feeling very excited at the prospect of being present at such an event. When the chairman's wife broke the champagne bottle over the bow of the ship we all cheered madly and applauded until our hands ached. When I looked round

53

at the workers there was so much pride on their faces that one would have thought they had built the ship single handed. It was a wonderful occasion and I was so glad that I had been allowed to be part of it.

Harry was an avid fan of the big bands that often came to Glasgow at that time. There was Billy Cotton, Doctor Crock and his Crackpots and Edmundo Ros, to name but a few. I had heard them on the radio but I had never seen them in a live show. Harry had a friend who was a part-time vocalist with one of the groups and usually could manage to get tickets for these events which he passed onto Harry.

As the name suggests Doctor Crock and his Crackpots was a band that had a comedy routine in the middle of their act. Sometimes they would leave the bandstand and mingle with the dancers, still playing their instruments and sometimes blowing trumpets into your ear. Billy Cotton followed much the same pattern, whereas Elmundo Ros played music mostly for tangos and rumbas and kept a very strict tempo. There was no nonsense with him. Sometimes with the Crackpots a couple of clowns would be let loose amongst the dancers causing absolute mayhem but it was all good fun and everybody had a good time.

Harry and I went out once or twice a week, sometimes to the cinema or just going for a walk if the weather was fine. It was a very casual thing; we enjoyed one another's company and Harry was such an easy-going chap that there was never any arguments or disagreements to spoil our friendship. I don't think it would have come to anything more than friendship between us as neither of us was looking for a serious relationship and we just went along with the flow.

A few weeks later Harry told me that his cousin who was in the Royal Marines was coming home on leave and asked me if I would mind if he came along with us on our outings. Of course I did not mind at all and when I suggested that I could bring my friend Nora along with us so that his cousin would not feel like the odd man out Harry agreed.

It turned out that John Wilkinson his cousin was coming home to be demobbed from the service on the grounds of ill health; he had caught malaria while serving abroad and had had quite a few recurring bouts, so it was thought unwise to send him abroad again. He arrived a few days later and Harry introduced us to each other. He was quite tall and fair-haired and looked very smart in his uniform. We made an appointment to go and see a film the following Saturday night and Nora my friend agreed to come along with us to make up the party. Of course we did not get much time to chat during the film but Nora told me later that John had a younger brother Joe who was studying in Rome for the priesthood and that his mother was a school teacher locally. Nora seemed very impressed with him and I thought that something might be happening between them. I certainly hoped so, because Nora was such a nice girl but did not seem to have much success with the boys. I had known her for years but in all that time I had never known her to have a serious relationship. We went out as a group quite a few times but I never really found it easy to talk much to John and left Nora to do much of the conversing. I kept hoping John would ask her out without Harry and I, but he never did. One evening when Nora and Harry had gone for refreshments for us I was taken aback when John suddenly said to me, 'Is it a serious thing with you and Harry?' I was very surprised at this question but answered that we were very good friends and why did he want to know? He said that he had not wanted to spoil things between us if it were serious but if it wasn't would I consider going out with him on my own? To say that I was surprised would be putting it mildly and for once in my life I was totally lost for words and mumbled something about I would think about it and let him know.

I did not say anything about this to Nora or Harry at the time but I knew that my answer would be in the negative as I did not feel that way about him and I did not want a serious relationship with anyone at that time. As it happened, on the following Saturday when we had arranged to meet Harry had a bad cold and was confined to bed, so it was just Nora and I who met at the cinema. We waited there for about half an hour but John did not appear. I was very relieved as it saved me answering the question and telling him my answer. Suddenly a tall young man appeared and approached us. 'Are one of you young ladies a Miss Dawson?'. When I said that I was he explained that he was John's brother Joe and that John had an attack of malaria and would not be able to meet us, but if we wished we could come home to the house for a cup of tea so that our night would not be entirely wasted. I was on the horns of a dilemma. Should I say no and appear to be ill mannered or boorish, or agree to go when all my instincts told me to turn and run? I looked at Nora and she nodded and said, 'Of course we will come, seeing as John is ill.' So the die was cast. The house was in Lambhill. a ten minute walk away, and when we got there Joe ushered us into the living room where his mother was waiting to greet us. She was rather a tall lady with grey hair and a rather severe expression, but she welcomed us and said that she was so pleased to meet us as she had heard so much about us and how kind we had been to John. We stayed for a cup of tea and when we were leaving she said she hoped we would call again when John was feeling better as he would appreciate having our company. I could only nod in agreement and make my escape as gracefully as possible. When we got outside I told Nora that I had intended to tell John that I was not going to see him again after tonight and that I had no romantic feelings for him, but Nora said that this would be cruel in the circumstances and that I should wait till he was on the mend again before I said anything to him. Against my better instincts I agreed to wait.

A few days later I received a letter from John apologising for being unable to meet us the previous Saturday and saying that he had been pleased that we had come to his house and met his mother and brother. He also said that he hoped that I had not been annoyed about his suggestion that we should go out as a couple. He did not want to rush me into making any decision about the future and was quite agreeable to be part of a foursome until that I felt I wanted to change things. Since he had come back from the services he had been so glad of our company as his previous friends had gone their separate ways and he had been very lonely until he met us. I could understand how he felt and as long as he was not going to rush things I did not mind going on as we had done previously. I wrote back and told him this and we agreed that we would meet on the following Saturday evening, the four of us as usual. This arrangement went on for a few weeks more and then something happened that changed everything. Harry had now finished his apprenticeship at the shipyards and was now a fully-trained carpenter and was looking for a job as a tradesman which would provide higher wages and better prospects. A friend of his mother who lived in London and knew about Harry's situation told her husband who worked in the construction business about it and he advised Harry that if he was willing to come to London he could guarantee him a job. The wages were quite good and he said that Harry could stay with them until such times that he found better lodgings. Harry was very excited about going to London and could not wait to get started, so he wrote back accepting the offer and a few days later he was onto pastures new. I was really pleased for him as he had always wanted to spread his wings and this was his chance to do so, but it left me feeling a little sad to be losing such a good friend and in a bit of a quandary about what to do about John. When I told my friend Nora about what had happened, she said that I had never really given myself a chance to get to know him, and that I should go out with him and see how things develop from there. As the fates seemed to be conspiring against me I agreed to give it a try and just to go with the flow.

John had been fortunate in getting his old job back. He had worked in a despatch department of a daily newspaper before joining the marines and when he was demobbed he had gone to see his previous employer and because of the shortage of manpower at that time and the fact that he was an experienced worker he was offered the job on the spot. The only drawback was that it was on constant night shift, every night except Saturday which was his one night off. The hours were from 6pm till 6am, but the wages were good and he was delighted to be back in the harness again. It meant that we could only go out the one night a week, but I always had Nora for company so I did not really mind. When I started to go out with John I discovered that what I thought had been his rather offhand manner was due to shyness and the fact that he had not a lot of self confidence with regards to the girls. But he was very attentive and caring and that made up for the lack of small talk. When I told my mother about him she was quite impressed. I think that the fact that his mother was a teacher and his brother was studying for the priesthood had a lot to do with it. I could just see her mind working: A nice steady lad and a good catholic family - what could be better for her daughter? Of course she wanted me to bring him home so she could meet him and when I did he met with both her and my father's approval. He was so polite and well mannered that there was not anything to merit their disapproval, which was a pleasant change for me as my previous relationships had not always run so smoothly.

Chapter Seven

At work lots of things had changed and out of our original staff only Mr Ross and I remained. Jessie had retired to look after her mother and the men were all working in the factories. I missed them all and the friendship that we had shared. At the end of the quarter all the member's accounts had to be cleared and their share book transactions had to tally with my ledger, on this occasion one of our member's books showed a difference of 30 shillings from the account in my ledger. I had to go over every single sale to find out what was causing the discrepancy. After a few hours work I finally discovered what was wrong and how the error had happened. For each sale the amount of that sale was added to the previous amount and brought down to as up to date amount which owed. After one such transaction a very badly written 5 had been brought forward as an 8 and this error had continued right through the rest of the quarter's total. So this meant the customer had been over charged by 30 shillings, when the customer came into the shop to clear her account I told her what had happened and said that she now owed 30 shillings less that which had been marked in her share book. As it happened the customers husband was serving in the forces and she had a couple of young children, so it must have been very hard for her to manage on a soldiers allowance and when she discovered that she had less to pay than she thought she promptly burst into tears and thanked me profusely. It really was not anything to do with me but she was so overjoyed that she would not listen to my protests and next day she appeared with a box of chocolates for me and insisted on me accepting them. I was just glad that now my totals had tallied, but of course I was still very happy at the outcome for her. 30 shillings or £1.50 in decimal money was an awful lot of money in those days.

The war was still dragging on after almost 4 years but now we were hitting back at the enemy on all fronts. The Air Force were bombing the main cities of Germany every night and the German people suffering in the same way as the Londoners had done previously, having their cities laid waste and their homes destroyed but this was war and the innocents suffered as well as the guilty. There were still strong rumours about a second front opening soon and we all wished it would happen so that we could finally see an end to this horrible war and the killing of our young brave men. At this time my sister Annie had got herself a new job in a factory and was working with a squad of brickies, all women, they took turns of having a night out in one another's houses, having a cup of tea and a sing song or in some cases bringing in a fortune teller to tell their fortunes or read the tea cups. One night it was my Sisters turn to act as host and she invited my friend Nora to come along and join the party. When we arrived the party was in full swing and when I saw my Sisters workmates I felt like walking out again. I had never seen such a rough looking bunch of women in my life, one of them was singing a song, a parody of one of the popular songs of that time and each verse was more ribald than the one before and Nora and I were becoming very embarrassed. My brother Joe had come to the house on some errand and walked into the house in the middle of the song and I don't know who was the most embarrassed, Joe or Nora and I. Joe just stood for a moment and then walked out into the kitchen with Nora and I at his heels. My sister was making tea for the company and when she saw us coming into the kitchen she asked what had happened and why we had left the party and when we told her she was most annoyed and said what would her workmates think of her when all her Family had walked out. Joe said that he could not care less what they had thought and if that if Annie could not bring her friends up to her level she should not let them drag her down to theirs. Annie was almost in tears but Nora and I agreed with Joe and we all left. My Sister had always been very ladylike and seeing her in this kind of company really upset us. However, very soon afterwards Annie left that job and we did not see that lot again. I was very thankful that my mother had not been invited as I dread to think what would have happened if she had been. She would probably told the singer to wash her mouth out with soap and water as she had told people this before if she heard them swearing them in her presence.

We always had a full house on a Sunday night. My father's brothers and their wives would come, the men to play to cards or to have a game of billiards and the women to gossip amongst themselves. My father had bought a small billiard table for the boys a few years previously and they had become quite proficient at playing. My father was a good player and so were his brothers. So the boys did not get much chance of playing on a Sunday night. My father took his game of cards very seriously and nobody was allowed to interrupt the game when he was playing. The children were there to be seen but definitely not heard. As usual my mother would make the tea for the company and provide the cakes and biscuits for the women while the men had their beer or whisky. On Sunday afternoon my mother would bake a few cakes or scones and make sandwiches, so there was always plenty to eat and everybody enjoyed themselves. John was a constant visitor on Sunday evenings; he was quite fond of a game of cards and played a passable game of billiards. So he fitted in quite well with the company. I was always made very welcome at his house and used to visit his mother a couple of times a week when he was at work. His father and his Uncle Pat were always present when I visited; his father was very friendly and chatted away to me but his uncle was rather quiet and hadn't much to say. I believe he had been staying with his sister, John's mother, for quite a few years since he had retired when he was quite young. He had a kind of stomach problem that made him unable to work. He had the sitting room-cum-bedroom as his own domain while John's mother and father slept in the kitchen which had a couple of double beds. Mr Wilkinson, or Jimmy as he asked me to call him, worked for the Corporation as a road mender and he was the exact opposite of his wife in every way; he was an ordinary, rather small, working-class man and he spoke like one and acted accordingly. She, on the other hand, was quite tall for a woman, and she looked like a school teacher and spoke like one. To me they appeared to be a most ill-assorted couple, but then they do say that opposites attract. By the way, I never called him Jimmy but always referred to him as 'Mr Wilkinson'. In my family, any adult was always called Mr or Mrs by us children except for relations who were addressed by their title, 'Auntie' or 'Uncle', but never by their Christian name alone.

John and I had been going out together for almost six months and he wanted us to become engaged on my 21st birthday, which was in a few months time: 11th May 1944. I spoke to my parents who were quite happy about this and I knew his mother would be pleased as she kept telling me that I was the daughter that she had always wanted to have. When my birthday arrived John gave me a pretty 3-stone diamond ring. It was the first expensive piece of jewellery that I had ever owned and I showed it off to all of my friends who were duly admiring and congratulated me. I would sit on the bus or tram with my hand against the window with my fingers splayed out so that the ring would show to its best advantage and everyone would be able to admire it. I suppose my friends must have been fed up listening to me extolling the beauty of my ring, but it was a new experience for me to be the centre of attraction and I certainly made the most of it.

All too soon however, it was back to the work-a -day world. The papers were now full of news about the Second Front which was said to be imminent, and finally it happened on the 6th of June 1944: D-Day, when our troops landed on the beaches in Normandy. Surely it could not be too long now until the war was over, especially now that the powerful countries of America and Russia were our allies. Most people in Britain knew a little about America, mostly through the movies from Hollywood but Russia was entirely unknown to most of us and the people of the country completely alien. From the sketchy information we had learned from our geography lessons at school we knew it was a vast country and for most of the year was covered in snow and ice, and that the criminals in their country were often sent to the labour camps in Siberia to serve their sentences. Very few survived to tell of their experiences.

We also knew from photographs that most of the citizens were shown with fur hats and coats to keep out the biting cold of the Russian winter. When they became our allies we learned a little more about them and their Premier, Joseph Stalin, who had been one of the main architects in the founding of the USSR, and in his search for power had exiled Trotsky his main protagonist and became leader. (Actually his rule was officially denounced by the USSR in 1956). In the photographs that we saw in the newspapers he looked quite an ordinary man, with a bushy black moustache and the broad face of a peasant. He looked so affable that his admirers in this country - of which there many - used to call him Uncle Joe. To them, and to us, ignorance was bliss and we also knew that in war we were forced to sleep with some strange bedfellows.

Speaking of strange bedfellows brings back to mind an occasion when I was a child and for a time we had been plagued by bed bugs. This was quite common in Glasgow at that time as most of the houses were very old and in badly need of repair. However, my mother was mortified that this should happen to her and tried everything she knew to try and get rid of them; she scrubbed the bed boards, laundered all the bedding, and shook out the mattress every morning, but still they kept coming. Until one day at her wits end, she decided to scrub the walls by the bed with disinfectant and finally discovered where they were coming from. We had a small holy picture on the wall above our bed and when my mother took it down she found that they adhesive which joined the picture to the frame had softened and was pitted with tiny holes where the bugs had been making a meal of the sweet sticky paste. The picture was burned with the frame, the walls disinfected and we had no more invited guests. My mother had thought that the picture was there to guard us through the night, but unfortunately any of the blessings that came from this were received by the bed bugs and not the family.

The Glaswegians had some strange expressions in their vocabulary which only a fellow citizen would understand. For example, if you were on a bus or a tram and the conductress - or clippy as she was called - asked you to vacate the vehicle for any reason she would shout, 'Com oan, get aff!' In English this meant, 'Come on and get off!', which was a contradiction in terms and impossible to do unless you were capable of doing two things at one time.

In another example, I was off work with flu and I was told to get a line from the doctor and to bring it back when I was able to begin working again. Was this a clothes line or a fishing line I wondered? It was neither of these; what the speaker intended to say was that I had to get a note from my doctor to say that I had been ill but now was fit again to work and that I should take this note back to my employer.

My mother also had some queer sayings which would mystify me. When someone or something had caused her outrage she would say that she was 'black affronted'. I could understand the 'affronted' part but why was it 'black'? Again, when we had goaded her beyond her endurance she would say that we had her 'heart and soul roasted', a condition which was incomprehensible to me but sounded really painful. When Christmas was near she would always say that it would be time for Sandy Claw to appear. Of course she meant Santa Clause but we did not dare correct her and Sandy Claw kept appearing every Christmas all through our childhood. Of all the mixed metaphors and strangled vowels that we were used to hearing my Aunt Mary Baxter, who was my mother's sister, capped the lot. After a leisurely morning window shopping at one of our big department stores she came home and announced that she had a lovely time walking through Hoey's windows. As the said window was of the plate glass kind this was indeed a very mean feat! These were the small threads that helped to make up the rich tapestry of our lives.

Chapter Eight

On the Home Front events were also moving quickly. After the excitement of the engagement was over, the next item on the agenda was the wedding and where and when it would take place. I had wanted to wait for a year or so but I was a lone voice crying in the wilderness. The trouble was that unless you were married there was no chance of getting your name on the Corporation housing list, and even then with no children a couple could wait for years for an offer of getting a rented house. Very few people at that time could afford to buy their own home, and I mentioned before that there was also a six-month waiting list for your furniture. Unless the couple were already married they were not considered as a priority case, and went to the back of the queue. So all things considered, everyone agreed that getting married as soon as possible was the next step forward. Everyone except me that is. I would like to have enjoyed the engagement period before the final commitment of marriage, but as I said I was a lone voice which went virtually unheard.

It was agreed at that time that the best time for getting married was during the summer months when the schools were on holiday and Joe would be home from college for a few weeks. So we duly went to see the priest to book the church for the ceremony. June and July were always the popular months for weddings and most of these were already booked up. So the date that we could get was for the 3rd of July which was only six weeks away and there were still all the preparations to be made. Booking a hall, arranging catering and of course finding a wedding dress. I could not imagine how all this could be accomplished in such a short time and I felt like I was on a merry-go-round and was being whirled around like a dervish, and wondered if I would ever get my feet on the ground again. By some means or other my mother managed to get a booking at the Co-op Hall, and the family put together the food coupons for a steak pie dinner. Betty gave me her wedding dress that had been in her wardrobe covered in plastic for almost three years since she had last worn it for her own wedding. It was a trifle long on me as she was a couple of inches taller than I was, but she took the hem up to make it the right length. Her silver wedding shoes also fitted after we put in some thick insoles and a pair of heel grips. I managed to buy a few clothing coupons to purchase a new suit and blouse for my going-away outfit and that was my wedding ensemble. In the meantime, Joe had written to the Pope's secretary to grant us a Papal Blessing which duly arrived a few weeks later, just in time for the ceremony. There is an old saying which goes, 'Something old, something new, something borrowed and something blue.' This is what the bride is supposed to have. As it happens I had all the essentials, plenty of old, something new, lots of borrowed items and I managed to buy a pair of unmentionables for myself.

On the big day I even had a guard of honour, a very grand name for six rather bewildered-looking guides from my patrol, who looked as if rather they would have been anywhere else rather than standing guard on me. Of course this had not been my idea but the captain of our troop, Charlotte, thought it would be a nice thing to do. Not one of her better ideas I fear. Nora, of course, was my bridesmaid and Joe was John's best man. John had managed to get a late booking for a small hotel in Rotheasay. So that concluded the wedding preparations, although I don't think it could be called the wedding of the year.

The hotel was rather nice, although the guests were mostly older people than we were. But the weather was very good and it was great to relax after all the frenzy of the previous weeks.

It was a pity that Joe could not perform the marriage ceremony as I would have wished, but he still had a year to go before his ordination although he was allowed to assist the priest and was present on the altar for most of the proceedings. It had been decided that we would stay with John's Uncle Jimmy, as he had a spare room. He had two sons, but the younger one, John, was in the Navy and only home occasionally when on leave. The older one, James, stayed in the family home with his father. I had met the two boys on a number of occasions and found John to be a charming young man, but James was rather a surly individual who for some reason seemed to resent his younger brother. Uncle Jimmy had said that they never got on well and this had been the main reason why John had joined the Navy.

Our stay in Uncle Jimmy's was only meant to be a stop-gap until we found something more suitable. It transpired we were still there after nearly a month had passed and I was getting really depressed with the situation. To make matters worse, I did not even have the distraction of work to take my mind of my problems. As was the usual procedure in the Co-op, married women had to vacate their jobs and although Mr Ross had asked for me to remain for a few weeks to train my successor that time was now over, and so after almost seven happy years I was not unemployed. It was hard to say goodbye to my friends and work mates after such a long time and I missed them dreadfully, but one must abide by the rules, so reluctantly I said my farewells and left.

As usual in an all-male household cleanliness was not a priority and Uncle Jimmy's house was no exception to the rule. They seemed to live in a perpetual clutter and as I now had plenty of time on my hands, I decided I would help out by cleaning out the cupboards. As it happened this was not one of my better ideas. I managed to attain some semblance of order in the food cupboards, but on tackling the ones underneath the sink I discovered an old tin full of crawling maggots. I did not know what the tin had originally contained and I did not wait to find out. I just wrapped up the tin and it's disgusting contents in some thick wrapping paper and deposited the whole lot in the bin in the back yard. When I told Uncle Jimmy what I had done he said that I would be in trouble when John came home on leave as I had thrown out his entire stock of maggots, which were his fishing bait. I did not know that John went fishing and even if I had known I would not have guessed that such degrading creatures could be used as bait to catch fish. I did not attempt to clean out any more cupboards while I was there.

It was a lonely time for me being stuck in a little pokey bedroom night after night when John had gone to work and I was on my own. Uncle Jimmy also worked most nights of the week and I did not seek out the company of James, as the few times when we did speak to one another I could tell he had been drinking and it scared me to be in the house on my own with him at night.

It all came to a head one night when he came home in a foul mood and obviously very drunk, and started arguing with Uncle Jimmy in the lounge. I sat in the bedroom shivering with nerves when suddenly there was the sound of blows being exchanged and Uncle Jimmy crying out in pain. I ran out of the bedroom and down the stairs and into the street. There was a telephone box at the corner, so I went in and dialled my mother-in-law's number. I could barely speak for crying but I somehow managed to tell her what had happened. She told me to stay in the phone box until Jimmy her husband came to collect me and bring me to their home. It seemed a long time to me but only about quarter of an hour or so before Jimmy appeared. I had never been so pleased to see his familiar face appearing outside that telephone kiosk. At that time very few people had phones in their home, most were professional people like doctors or lawyers. I was so glad that night that my mother in law was one of the few that were fortunate enough to posses that amenity.

As soon as we arrived at the house my mother-in-law phoned John at work and told him to come home after his shift had finished and not to go to Uncle Jimmy's house. My father-in-law went back to check on Jimmy to see if he was alright. I was a little worried about him going back there with James in the mood that he was in. My mother-in-law had said that he, my father-in-law, had been a good boxer in his day and could still handle himself in that department. I was surprised to hear this but then I knew next to nothing about what he had been like when he was young. All I knew was that he had been a good player of the fiddle and my mother-in-law had met him at one of the dances where he was playing. I realised that living in the shadow of his wife's more dominant personality had reduced him to the person he had then become, a rather insignificant figure who faded into the background when she was around. But I also realised that he also must have had dreams and hopes of his own when he was younger, and maybe in different circumstances these would have been realised, and after that night I saw him a different light than I had previously.

He returned to the house with Uncle Jimmy in tow about half an hour later and told us that Jimmy had run out of the house after I had left. Uncle Jimmy's face was slightly bruised but he was not badly hurt, although still very shaken after his experience. I think what hurt him most was the fact that his son was the cause of the whole sordid affair, and that he had sunk so low as to attack his own father. And worst of all, I had been there when it happened. We found out later that the quarrel had started because the girl that James was friendly with had been evicted from her house because of arrears and James had told his father that he wanted her to move into the house with him. Uncle Jimmy had refused immediately to consider this and that was when the argument escalated into violence. I don't know if or when James returned to the house but I did not see him again, and the whole affair was hushed up and never spoken about. It was not a very promising start to our married life and although we were much more comfortable in my in-laws' home, I still felt very guilty about Uncle Pat being ousted from his little domain to accommodate us and was not sleeping in the kitchen in one of the double beds and had lost most of the privacy he had formerly enjoyed.

My mother-in-law was kindness itself, but I did not feel comfortable about the upset that we were causing by staying there. My mother knew that I was unhappy with the situation and would have liked us to stay in her house, but with John, Peter and Chrissie still at home there simply was not room for us there either. So we just had to stay where we were in the meantime until something turned up to ease the situation.

In the meantime, I had taken a part time job in the dairy next door to my mother-in-law's house, and as she would not take any rent money from us it enabled us to save a little for the time we would be allocated a rented house.

We had been married for a few months when we got the offer of a single apartment at Queen's Cross in the Maryhill district of Glasgow. When we went to view it my heart sank. It was a tiny kitchen with a bed set into the wall, a tiny window which looked into the back yard, an outside toilet, and a sink with a cold water tap and a coal fire. But at least it was our own and we were grateful for that. Of course we had no furniture yet although we had ordered a dining table, chairs and a sideboard, but these items would not be delivered for a few months yet. So we had to buy a cheap wooden kitchen table and chairs. My parents bought linoleum for the floor and a small rug for the front of the fireplace. My father made us a wooden stool as he had done for Annie and Joe when they got married and my in-laws provided the money for the kitchen utensils that we needed, like cutlery, china, kettle, teapot etc. It does not sound a lot but I guess many couples had started married life with a lot less, and as we had also received bedding, towels and such items as wedding presents, we had enough to give us a start at making a home. I felt that I had turned full circle and I was not back in the surroundings in which I had started out. The loneliness was the worst thing of all, every night on my own with no one to talk to and nothing to look at except four walls and the view of a dismal backyard. This sounds very self pitying but that was how I felt at the time.

There was another door on the landing so I guessed that I must have a neighbour but I had not seen or heard any signs of occupancy up till the present, however a few days later I bumped into a lady on my way to the back yard who turned out to be my neighbour, a Miss Grant. We introduced ourselves and she seemed a very nice person and I was glad to know that I had someone next door to me, and that I was not entirely alone, especially at night. She told me that she too was on her own in the house and she was as pleased as I was to have had someone next door. She was in her late 30s or so, but I noticed that her hands were slightly twisted and she explained that she had severe arthritis and couldn't do anything very strenuous as she was in a lot of pain most of the time and that her other joints were also affected by the arthritis.

I said that she would be welcome to visit me at any time for a cup of tea and she accepted immediately, so I guess she must have been a bit lonely too. She came in most nights after that when John had gone to work, and her visits made all the difference to me as I no longer felt so isolated.

There was a small convenience store at the bottom of our street and I noticed when I passed it one day that they had a card in the window saying that there was a vacancy for a part-time shop assistant. So I went in and applied for the job and was told to start right away. It was just a few hours in the mornings, which suited me fine. So once again I was one of the employed. I felt that things were looking up at last and when I thought of Miss Grant and the difficulties she had in moving around and the pain she was suffering I felt ashamed of myself for my self pity. I was young and healthy and I should be grateful for that. I had a lot to be thankful for and should learn to count my blessings instead of bemoaning my fate.

Chapter Nine

The street where I lived Bonawe Street was only a few minutes' walk away from the Maryhill greyhound race track, and as my brother Peter and his friends were avid followers of the sport they used to come to my house for tea before going on to the track meetings. I looked forward to their visits as I enjoyed the company and also I could catch up on all the family gossip.

One night on one of these visits I was alarmed to hear that my mother was ill with pleurisy and was confined to the house. I had never known my mother to be ill or even to complain of as much of as a headache. So I knew that it must be serious for her to be confined to bed. I decided that I would go home to see how I could help out and to discover how serious her illness really was. When I arrived home I discovered that she was now over the worst and on the mend, but I stayed there for a few days in order to do the shopping and the housework. When she was in pain my father had painted the affected part with iodine - a remedy for all ills at that time - but had made matters worse by overdoing it and causing the skin to burn, which had been a setback to her recovery. I am sure my mother must had a few choice words to say when this happened but at least she was now getting better and I could go back to my own house with an easier mind. When I returned to Maryhill I found to my horror that my door was all barricaded up and a notice pinned to it which read, 'Would owner please report to Maryhill Police station on return'. I was totally shocked and could not think what had happened in my absence. I knocked on Miss Grant's door to see if she could give me an explanation and she told me that shortly after I had left she had noticed that my door was not properly closed and was afraid of someone breaking in. She had tried to close it herself but the lock must have slipped and she could not manage it, so she had reported it to the police station and someone had come and boarded it up and left a notice for me to find when I returned.

John had been due for a few days' holiday so I had suggested that he should stay with his family while I was away as I did not know how long I would be needed at home. It had not occurred to me to leave my parents' address, so there was no way they could contact me. I duly went to the police station and received a lecture and was told not to be careless in the future, but a policeman did come back with me to remove the barricade so that I could gain entry to my house. I felt a proper idiot for being the cause of so much bother but I suppose with my record of things never going smoothly I guessed this was par for the course.

When I was young and the seasons were more predictable, June was always considered to be the best month for fair weather. But even then occasionally there would sometimes be days when the sun would hide behind the clouds, the rain would pour down and the sky would be black and forbidding. A little like life really when suddenly a cherished dream could be shattered and an expected triumph reduced to ashes. When on occasion things did not go to plan, my mother as usual had a saying of her own. After any disappointment, when things had not turned out as well she had hoped, she would say, 'Ay yes, it's chilly for June'. On the other side of the coin, even in the darkest days of December occasionally the sun would break through and you would realise that winter would not last forever and summer would come again.

My mother-in-law was a very devout Catholic, and over and above teaching the 3 Rs it was also she who prepared the children in her class for their First Holy Communion and Confirmation. She knew all the Latin responses for the prayers said during the mass, as at that time all masses were conducted in Latin, the ancient language of the church. Even the little altar boys, or servers as they were called, had to learn the Latin responses before they could serve at the altar. On a few occasions if the server had not turned up before Mass, my mother-in-law would act as a stand-in, but she was not allowed to appear on the altar, only to serve outside the altar rails. Now it is quite common for girls to act as servers but at that time this was unheard of. On the day of the first communicants my mother-in-law always had a tin of talcum powder nearby and she would cover her hands with this in case she might mark the children's dresses with perspiration as she was helping them to dress. No mother could have been prouder of their children than she was of her pupils. They say that teaching is not only a job but a vocation and in her case this was certainly true.

Joe and John had also served on the altar when they were younger and Joe told me that when he was learning the Latin responses, there was a part of the mass where they had to confess their sins. The Latin words for this were: mea culpa, mea culpa, mea maxima culpa. In English this meant: through my fault, through my fault, and through my most grievous fault. He used to say under his breath: me a cowboy, me a cowboy, me a Mexican cowboy. So not very much a Holy Joe after all, but then boys will be boys.

I think my mother-in-law would have been a happier person if she had had a large family instead of just the two boys, and I know she hoped one day to have lots of grandchildren she could spoil. Speaking of grandparents, I haven't a very clear picture of mine. I remember vaguely of being taken to my father's parents' house when I was quite young and being slightly in awe of these two old people who were dressed entirely in black clothes and looked to a small child very stern and forbidding. I have a slightly clearer and more cheerful memory of my mother's parents' house. My granddad Burns was a small, fat, cheery man who always wore a big silver watch chain round his middle, and he would let us play with it when we sat on his knee. He stayed with his son and daughter, my Uncle James and Aunt Mary, as my Grandma Burns had died many years before. My Aunt Mary Baxter had married rather late in life to a man much older than herself. She was very plain woman and rather childish in some ways, and it was difficult to believe that she and my mother were sisters. They were so unlike each other in every way. There was one child from this marriage, a boy who did very well at school, went onto further studies at night school and later on in life passed all his tests to become a draughtsman. So from very unpromising beginnings he had achieved his goal and surprised us all. His father did not live to share in his success, but my Aunt Mary did and in being a dutiful son he ensured that his mother had a happier and more affluent old age than she had ever dreamed of.

At that time large families were the norm. My father had seven brothers, two of whom were twins, and one sister. My mother had three sisters and one brother, plus a few more that had died in infancy. Two of her siblings were also twins, so there were twins on both sides of our family. My mother's brother Edward, who I have not mentioned before, was a very handsome man and a bit of a rogue with the ladies. As my mother often said, he led his wife a bit of a merry dance. My mother also had a sister Annie who was the youngest of the family. Annie was married to a man who was a cobbler to trade, not a very profitable occupation in those days, and I know that my mother often gave her money to help her out. On one occasion after the birth of one of her children, of which she had many, she came to visit my mother to ask if she could borrow a coat to wear when she took her baby out for the first time after the birth, as she was so ashamed to be seen without a decent thing to wear. My mother was the oldest of her family and she was the one they all turned to when in need, and I don't think that they were ever refused her help. Now in more affluent times not many people realise how hard life was for people at that time, before the war brought some prosperity and jobs were plentiful after the depression of the early 1930's. It's tragic to realise that it takes a war with all the suffering this entails and the loss of so many young lives to bring this about.

On the 6th June 1944, The Second Front, or D-Day as it was known, began.

On 20th January 1945 the RAF dropped 2,300 tonnes of bombs on Berlin and a few days later on the Russian front, Stalingrad was relieved after a two- year siege.

On the 28th April 1945 Mussolini was murdered by Italian partisans and his body put on display in Milan. On 30th April 1945 Hitler committed suicide in his bunker in Berlin. A few months earlier US troops had liberated the concentration camp a Dachau, and the camps at Belsen and Buchenwald had been liberated earlier in the month. The liberators were appalled at what they discovered. The sheer scale of the Holocaust was undeniable despite the last minute attempt by the Germans at a cover up. An estimated six million Jews, plus hundreds of thousands of others, had lost their lives. When the pictures of the camp survivors appeared in the newspapers the world recoiled in horror. As the men stumbled out to freedom with shaven heads, faces gaunt and emaciated and limbs resembling matchsticks they bore no resemblance to human beings. Of all the atrocities committed in war - and there were many - surely this must have been the worst example of man's inhumanity to his fellow man!

On the 5th of May 1945 Germany accepts unconditional surrender and on the 8th of May 1945 the Armistice was signed. At last, after almost six years of war in Europe, we were at peace. Of course, we were still in a state of war with Japan, but at least we could now see the light at the end of the tunnel and we rejoiced at what had been achieved so far. When the news of the surrender of the German Army was announced, the people were exultant with joy and relief. Strangers in the street embraced each other and the King and Queen came out onto the balcony of Buckingham Palace to greet the crowds who had gathered there. The young Princesses Elizabeth and Margaret mixed with the crowd to share in their jubilation.

Street parties were set up for the children, benches and tables were begged and borrowed from schools and churches, and rations were pulled so the children could enjoy a feast of celebration after the years of austerity. Even an old piano was wheeled out onto the street and all the old war songs were sung with gusto. It was a wonderful time and everyone uttered a prayer of gratitude that they had survived the horrors of the war and had been spared to enjoy this day of freedom.

On the 2nd August British troops liberated Burma and four days later a US Atomic bomb destroyed the city of Hiroshima killing 78,000 people. This was followed by a more powerful A-bomb on Nagasaki. On the 9th August, Japan accepted unconditional surrender, including the removal from power of the Emperor Hirohito. The formal surrender was signed on the 2nd September 1945. So the war was now over on all fronts. Thanks Be To God.

Chapter Ten

In the post-war period, things were not much easier on the home front in Britain. Rationing was still very severe and even in 1947, two years after the war, there were more food shortages than there had been during the hostilities. This, combined with a shortage of fuel and two severe winters in succession made life very difficult for the population.

On a personal level none of these things affected me very greatly. My only worry was about my father, who was very ill and had been for quite a few months. We had not realised how seriously ill he was as he had carried on working as usual until he was physically unable to do so. We found out that he had throat cancer and it was inoperable. Eventually he was taken to hospital. We visited him every day but towards the end he did not even know we were there as he was kept in a coma for most of the time under the influence of morphine. The cancer was now spreading towards the brain and the pain was intense. My mother was sent for when the end was near and the family went with her to say their goodbyes. Peter was at work when the message came so he was late in arriving at the hospital. My father asked my mother to kiss him goodbye on the cheek but not to touch him on the mouth. We were in floods of tears and we thought then that he had gone, but he rallied slightly and asked for Peter. My mother explained that he was on his way, and shortly afterwards he arrived. When my father saw him he reached under his pillow and took out his rosary beads and pen knife which he always carried and gave them to Peter after which he seemed to relax. Suddenly his eyes turned to the corner of the room and a big smile transformed his face, smoothing all the pain lines away, and then he was gone. My mother said that she was sure that he had seen James, his first-born son, and now he was with him and at peace. Who were we to refute this belief. It was a beautiful sunny day in August 1947 when my father was buried. I could not understand how the sun could shine and the people could go about their usual business as if nothing had happened when my whole world had collapsed around me and my father was gone forever.

When the cortege left the house my young sister was screaming and shouting for her dad and grabbing at the curtains on the window so tight that she had pulled them right down. It was expected for us to hold a wake for my father, but it was a harrowing event for us all, especially my mother. She made us promise that when it was her time to go there would be no wake for her, and we kept that promise. My father was 62 years of age when he died, but my mother lived for another 11 years although for her and for the family, life would never be the same again.

My brother John, much to everyone's surprise, had decided a few years previously that he was going to join the Mill Hill Fathers, who were based in London. He was not becoming a monk, but he was joining as a lay-brother, helping by working in the gardens or the kitchen or wherever he might be needed. John had always had been a bit of a home-bird, and it came as a big surprise to us that he was leaving home, and especially for the fact that he would be working in a monastery. But then John had always been a bit of a mystery to the rest of us, so we should not have been too surprised. He seemed to settle in very well and his letters home were quite cheerful and full of his activities. He had been away from home for over a year when my father had died, and when my mother wrote to tell him the sad news he wrote back immediately to say he was coming home as he felt that he would be needed with my father gone. My mother tried to dissuade him but to no avail. To be truthful, she was pleased that he had settled so well in his new life as she had always worried about him as he was a bit of a loner and not so resilient as the rest of us. He had no interest in girls and she worried about what would happen to him when she had gone and who would take care of him. As I said he had made up his mind to come home and that was his decision to make so she had to agree with his wishes and give in graciously.

In my family my father had been the head and my mother the heart and together they provided the glue that blended our family together as a unit. Now with that bond slightly loosened a little of that closeness had gone.

At the beginning of 1948 my mother-in-law had brought home a letter which had been sent round the school asking for volunteers who were willing to take a French orphan into their homes for a few weeks to give them a holiday. They were being brought into the school in a few days time and any interested party could come and see the children and chose one to take home with them. All these children had lost a parent during the war mostly a father and needed a break away from home. My mother-in-law wondered if I would be interested, and as I had been recently allocated a room and kitchen in Springburn and now had an extra bedroom, and as it was only for a few weeks I agreed. After four years of marriage I still had no children and I thought it would be nice to have a bit of company in our home. A few days later I went to the school and picked a little girl, a pretty child with dark hair and lovely brown eyes. Her name was Michelle Le Bars and she was 11 years old and came from Brest in Northern France. Her clothes were spotlessly clean but a little worn, so the first thing we did was to take her shopping for new clothes and shoes. At that time the fashion for little girls was white ankle-socks and black patent leather shoes with an ankle strap. These were called baby peggy shoes, so we bought her these and her eyes lit up when she put them on and afterwards she would not go out unless she was wearing them. I suppose even at that early age the love of fashion that the French were famous for was already part of her in her love for fashion and wearing pretty things. She stayed with us for the whole time that they remained in Britain, about four weeks in all. When it was time for her to go home we gave her presents for mother and a baby doll for her young sister, and when she arrived she sent us a thank you letter and a photograph of her sister with the doll which she had called Janette. This was the French version of my name and I was very touched by the thought. We corresponded for a while but after a time the letters stopped coming as usually happens, but it was good experience for me and I hope she felt the same. I still think of her sometimes and wonder if she is happy.

At the end of the war in 1945, television was in its infancy and only had a small number of viewers who were fortunate enough to possess a set. By the end of the early 1950's there were millions of TV sets taking pride of place in British homes. At the beginning there was not very much to look at, there were only a few programmes each day and these were mostly for the children. There were gaps of a few hours between each programme, but it was such a novelty being able to sit in your own home and watch moving pictures that we watched anything that moved on the screen. No wonder it was called a goggle box!

My brother John had bought a television supposedly for my mother's benefit, but it proved a mixed blessing to her as very few of our neighbours had a set and if there was anything interesting showing John would invite them to come in and watch the programme.

Sometimes there would be about a dozen people crowded into the lounge and the job of supplying refreshments usually fell on my mother's shoulders. So nothing changed there.

There were lots of things happening on the home front. The government relaxed food controls in 1948 and in 1949 clothes rationing ended also. In 1948 the National Health Service came into effect, and the Olympic Games were held in London. The Festival of Britain was held in 1951. In 1952 King George VIth died and was succeeded by his daughter Princess Elizabeth. Her coronation took place in June 1953 and was televised and watched by millions all over the world. So we now had a Queen, Elizabeth IInd, on the throne.

There was not much in life that held any fear for my mother. She took most things in her stride except for anything that threatened the well being of her family. But there was one thing that struck terror into her heart, and that was a thunder and lightning storm. We had a long windowless hall and when there was a storm on, my mother would sit there on a stool facing the wall and would not budge until it was all over. There were no meals made or any work done until things were back to normal. She couldn't see the lightning because there was no window, but if there was a clap of thunder she would run in and flush the toilet to cover the noise. She blamed her fear on the time she worked in the laundry, as the manageress would not let them do any work if there was storm brewing. There were not allowed to use irons or mangles and had to sit quietly until it was all over. We could have understood this if these appliances had been electrical but they weren't. The manageress was so terrified she was not taking any chances. This fear rubbed off on her workers and never left my mother.

My brothers Peter and John would sit in the bedroom and watch the lightning flash across the sky and listen to the thunder while my mother sat mute with terror and stared at the wall. One night when there was a really bad electrical storm which lasted for hours she had all us children round the bed saying the rosary and praying for a safe deliverance. We used to laugh at this afterwards but to my mother it was a very real terror and one she never got over. Surprisingly enough it never really affected any of us in later life which was fortunate as one person with this phobia was enough for any family.

Since I had moved house I was now working in the cash desk in a big department store in town, Arnott and Simpsons, usually in the gents' department but I was also the relief cashier for other departments when required. I liked my job because it gave me a bit of variety and as it was a busy store the hours passed quickly. In the gents' department we had all kinds of customers, from businessmen buying suits and shirts to lowly sailors just off the boats and with a few pounds to spend on trousers socks and underwear and so on. The lowest order of the sailors were called coolies and it was these people who did all the menial jobs on the ships and were looked down on by their shipmates. They were mostly coloured people or Chinese. The manager of our department told me that when they came to be measured for suits or trousers their underwear would have put the business men's under garments to shame as they were so spotlessly clean. As they say, you should never judge a book by its cover.

I had become friendly with a girl in one of the other departments. Her name was Sheila and she was a bit posh, but a very nice girl. She lived in a big house in Burnside, a prosperous suburb of Glasgow. Her father was a manager in one of the big credit companies and when I stayed in Bonawe Street I had asked her to tea in my house one evening when we were going to see a film. My house was near to the picture house and it saved her a journey. When she walked into the kitchen she said, 'Oh what a dinky little place you have got, just like a dolls house'. The trouble was that I was not a doll, but she was so used to living in a spacious environment that it was novelty to her that anyone would anyone would be able to eat, live and sleep in the one room. In her case ignorance was bliss.

As I have said, I had been allocated a house in Springburn: a room and kitchen in Down Street, a misnomer if there ever was one, as my house was at the top of two steep hills just off the main road.

When I was going to work in the mornings I used to pass an old man coming up the hill with his morning paper. We would say good morning as I was running past him to catch my bus to work. One morning as we passed each other he said, 'Lassie, lassie you will have to slow down or you will be running out of petrol'. But leaving everything to the last minute had always been my habit and I am afraid I still have not changed my ways.

My house was a big improvement on the previous one as I had a larger kitchen and an extra bedroom, but there was a fly in the ointment: I was living next door to the original neighbours from hell. The other people in the flats were ordinary, decent hard-working people, but the two men next door did not fit into that category at all. They were father and son and they fought and argued from morning till night. I heard from the other neighbours that the mother had died recently and the house had been given to her son who had stayed with her at the time she died. They say that she was nice old lady who lived quietly and gave no trouble to anyone, but when she died her grandson had moved in with his father and that was when the trouble started. They were both heavy drinkers and Friday nights were a nightmare when, drunk and incapable, they would stagger upstairs, bang doors, shout and swear at each other with things usually ending up in fight between them. I would sit in my kitchen terrified, listening to them knocking one

86

another up and down their hall and praying that they would not come to my door. It would be well after midnight before things would quieten down and even then I would be afraid to go to bed in case things would start up again.

I had moaned about the lack of space in my previous house but at least it had been quiet and I had a nice neighbour, but it seemed now that I had jumped from the frying pan into the fire and I would have given anything to be back in my doll's house again.

There was a nice couple who stayed in the flat below me, a Mr and Mrs Downie and their young daughter. He was a dental mechanic and she was a housewife. I used to see Mr. Downie in the mornings at the bus stop when we were going to work as we both worked in town. He was a really nice man and we would have a chat while we waited on the bus. I told him about my neighbours and he agreed with me that it was an awful state of affairs, but what could we do about it. He and his wife were as unhappy about the situation as I was but these people were not the type you could reason with and as long as they kept the trouble in their own home and did not interfere with anyone else the police would do nothing about it. So we just had to grin and bear it.

At this time stiletto heels were very fashionable and I had bought a pair of shoes with these pointed heels. I was talking to Mrs Downie one day when we passed on the stairs and she was joking about the noise I was making walking up and down my kitchen floor and suggesting that I should buy a pair of slipper to deaden the noise. I had never worn slippers but I agreed to buy a pair to please her. We were laughing about this and the younger man from next door passed us going downstairs. I did not think anything about this at the time, but that night there was knock on my door and when I opened it he was standing there drunk as usual and demanding to know why my neighbour and I had been laughing at him. I tried to explain that we had not been talking about him at all, but I could see that he did not believe me and twice more that night he came asking the same question. I was becoming very frightened but eventually he left muttering under his breath and calling me a few choice names. I went downstairs to warn Mrs. Downie about what had happened. She told me to stay in her house until Frank her husband came home and when he did they came upstairs with me and stayed until things were quiet again. He did not come again that night and to my relief a few weeks later he and his father were evicted from the house for non-payment of rent, which had not been paid since the mother died. So peace reigned again.

My brothers John and Peter were still living at home with my mother, both still single and showing no signs of settling down, but my young sister Chris had started courting, a young man called David Greer who lived with his widowed mother and an older brother. Chris, as she was now known by her friends, had started work as a telephone operator in the western area of Glasgow. When she was training for the job my mother said that she used to drive them mad when she was rehearsing what she had been taught. Like counting '1, 2, 3, 4, 5' or 'I am trying to connect you' or 'this line is busy could you call later', with all this spoken in a very posh voice and repeated over and over again.

David had just recently been demobbed from the Army where he had served in the Military Police and it soon became clear that this was a serious relationship, so after a few weeks my mother invited him for tea. I had already met him and found him a very nice and polite young man. He was a few years older than Chris but that was a good thing in many ways as the grief of my father's death was still quite raw and she needed somebody steady and reliable whom she could depend on, and he was that type of person. There was one obstacle in the way: he was not a Catholic. In fact he belonged to The Church of Scotland and this was fact worried my mother because the members of that Church were very much opposed to the Catholic teachings and beliefs. But Chris said she had made it quite clear to David that unless he took instruction in her faith and became a Catholic there would be no relationship between them. At that time it was quite unusual for a man to change his religion for the sake of a woman, although plenty of women gave up their faith to adopt the religion of their future husband. The biggest hurdle for a man to overcome was that any children of the marriage had to be brought up as Catholics and this was not an easy decision for a man to promise to abide by. But Chris was a very determined young woman. She had made her position clear and left the decision up to him to make for himself. He agreed to go for instructions but we all had our misgivings whether he would carry it through, especially as his mother was so against it and relations must have been very strained between them. However, David did his course of instructions and was eventually received into the Catholic Church and was a staunch member of that church for the rest of his life. In truth, as sometimes happens, he was more devout to its teachings than others like us who had been born into the faith. Later on when he retired from work it was he who read the lessons at Sunday Mass. So Chris's faith in his resolve and determination had not been misplaced and the family's doubts had been proved to be groundless.

Joe my oldest brother had now left the Merchant Navy and was at present working on dredging work in Arromanches in France salvaging boats that had been sunk during the war. This work proved to be a long term contract so after a few months Betty joined him there. After more than seven years of married life they still had no children, although I heard later there had been a miscarriage early on in their marriage. My mother did not discuss these private matters in the house and I only heard about this many years later from a different source.

My oldest sister Annie had three children, one girl and two boys. The eldest one, Rose, was now approaching her teens, so my mother had been a grandmother for quite a few years. Annie and Jimmy were still doing well and both working, but a few years previously Jimmy had been very ill and for a short time we thought we were going to lose him. He had contracted a disease of the inner ear, an inflammatory condition, and the pain was so intense that he was literally climbing the walls in agony. Eventually he had to undergo an operation and for a few days afterwards it was touch-and-go whether he would live or die. But eventually he recovered although he was left slightly deaf in one ear.

Annie my sister was not aging gracefully. She had been a pretty young woman and still had the lovely skin and blue eyes like my mother, but her love of sweet things like chocolate and cakes had caused her weight to balloon and she looked much older than an a woman in her early forties. She had never used make up or worn very fashionable clothes and seemed to be quite happy to settle into middle age before her time. Unlike me she had always been very well endowed in the bust department and although I had often wished for a more womanly figure I was quite resigned to the fact that I would never be a sex symbol and was quite prepared to put up with my shortcomings in that department. I was still very slim and one day when my mother and I were watching a neighbour's daughter leaving the house to get married the neighbours were standing with us and one of them made a remark that really put the cat amongst the pigeons. I was wearing a tight dress that made me look even thinner than usual and the neighbour said to my mother, 'Is your daughter well enough? She looks very thin to me'. I was taken to the doctor the next day insisting that I was fine and did not need a doctor, but my mother said if the neighbours were concerned about my health it was up to her to do something about it, so I had to go. The doctor thoroughly examined me and when he was finished he said to my mother, 'There is absolutely nothing wrong with her. She is thin, but very wiry and very fit'. I felt like saying to my mother, 'I told you so', but of course I did not dare. Looking back I can understand my mother's feelings as with tuberculosis so prevalent at that time, even an innocent remark like our neighbour had made could cause a lot of worry. But now at least she could believe that her fears were groundless.

My Sister Chris and David were married in St. Theresa's Church on the 5ᵗʰ January 1949, one day before her 20ᵗʰ birthday. It was quite a big occasion with the reception held at the Cadoro Restaurant in town which catered mostly for weddings and grand occasions. My cousin Betty, daughter of my Aunt Mary Dawson, was bridesmaid, David's brother was his best man and the bride was given away by my brother John standing in for my father. Their honeymoon was spent in a hotel in Perthshire. Chris told me later that she felt faint after the ceremony, which was understandable as it was a bitterly cold morning and she had had nothing to eat since the night before. This was the usual procedure at that time; anyone taking communion fasted from midnight until after taking the host. She said that she was taken into the sacristy of the church and the priest gave her a small glass of brandy to revive her. What some people will do for a free drink.

Speaking of St. Theresa's church, before I was married Nora and I used to collect the quarterly church collection for Father Murphy, one of the Curates at that time. We had five priests serving in our parish. The parish priest was Father Conlan, a saint of a man who was loved by all his parishioners. There was also Father

McGuran, Father McGrory, Father Murphy, and the youngest one who was just ordained was Father Wilson. There were five masses on a Sunday, starting at 7am with the last one at 12 noon, all well-attended by the congregation. The Sunday collection consisted mostly of coppers with an occasional three penny piece or sixpence offered by the better-off people of the parish. The children were given a penny to put in the plate, but it was not unusual to see the adults put in a small piece of silver and take out some coppers in return. The quarterly collection was for any repairs needed for the church and the usual amount expected was five shillings every quarter.

Some people could not afford that amount at one time and preferred to pay it a little each week, and these were the people that I used to visit every Sunday afternoon. One of these families was very poor and we had told them that they did not have to pay anything at all, but the woman insisted that she did not want to be different from anyone else and wished to pay her dues to the church. So we had to abide by her wishes. As I have said, they were very poor and their house was very sparsely furnished, but there was always a cheery fire burning and the woman always had a smile on her face when we called. She had three small children and although perhaps they were not the cleanest of their kind they were nonetheless always happy and full of life. There was an old tin bath in the middle of the floor with next week's laundry in it and the kids would be jumping out and in and shouting at the tops of their voices as they played. Their mother would insist that we took a cup of tea with her and of course we could not hurt her feelings by refusing. We did not know what kind of state her kitchen was in, but she did make some lovely fruit slices, full of currants and raisins and covered with puff pastry, and as we were young with healthy appetites we did not ask any questions and just tucked in and enjoyed them.

Perhaps that family did not have much of the worldly goods but the children were healthy, warm and well-fed, and most of all they were loved. So what else does a child require from life than these things?

As I said, we had five priests in our parish, all nice ordinary people except perhaps for Father McCrery who had served as a Padre with the forces during the war and had been demobbed suffering from slight shell-shock. He acted quite normally most of the time but occasionally he was very, very irritable and a bit forgetful, but it did not interfere with him performing his priestly duties, and as he was in a safe, quiet environment it was the right place for him to regain his health again. Father Wilson was a handsome young man and had two lovely dimples that showed when he smiled. The young girls in the parish used to run after him, trying to attract his special attention, but he would just smile and treat us all the same. Contrary to the belief that Catholics and Protestants were bitter enemies, Father Conlan and the local Minister of the Protestant church were great friends and used to play golf together every week. At that time Catholic priests did not have many luxuries in their life. They had their board and lodgings supplied by the church, but everything else, such as clothes and so on, were usually provided for by their parents. It was not unusual to see a priest with down-at-heel footwear, or shiny trousers due to constant wear. Most of the clergy at that time wore a long black cloak called a soutine which buttoned up from the neck to the feet, and like charity these covered a multitude of sins. They also wore a square cap called a beretta on their head. You very seldom see those articles worn these days, although they still exist and are occasionally worn by some of the older priests.

At the present time most priests have cars or access to one, but at that time the priest walked everywhere or depended on public transport, and only a fortunate few who had wealthy parents or belonged to a prosperous parish church could hope to attain such luxuries. St. Theresa's parish certainly did not fit into that category. Unlike nowadays we had a plentiful supply of young men entering the priesthood. Most of these came from Ireland where in a large family there was usually one son expected to join the church and their parents regarded this as a blessing and a privilege. Alas, those days are long gone, and now there is usually only priest for each parish and most of these have to provide cover for other Catholic churches in their area if they are needed. The Catholic churches still keep going but it is now a daily struggle to survive due to the shortage of priests. In these modern times where money and power are gods, being a priest is in the lowest pile of jobs which young career-minded people aspire to achieve.

My brother-in-law Joe was now ordained as a curate in a working class parish in Glasgow. His ordination was an unforgettable experience. There were three young men taking their vows on the same day, and when it came to that part of the ceremony where they all lay prostrate on the altar and offered themselves and their work to God, the tears were streaming down my face. They were all so young and innocent in the ways of the world. They would never be able to marry or have children, but the pride on their faces when they were blessed by the Bishop and welcomed into the church as priests was a wonderful thing to behold. The parents of the young men including my parents-in-law had joined together to celebrate the occasion by holding a lunch after the ceremony in one of the large restaurants in town. My mother and father had also been invited and we had a wonderful day with a four-course lunch, with wine after each course and speeches by the three young priests thanking their parents and families for their contribution in helping them to achieve their dream of becoming a priest and for making that dream become a reality. When Father Joe made his speech he too gave thanks to his parents and to his brother John and his sister Netta: me, which I thought was a lovely touch.

We had put together to buy him his chalice which he would use when he celebrated his masses throughout his priesthood. It was a wonderful day for him and for us and certainly an unforgettable one for me and my parents also.

Chapter Eleven

The stork had been working overtime recently after a long period of absence, as when Betty returned from her visit to Arromanches it was to announce that she was pregnant, and a few weeks after returning from her honeymoon my sister Chris found out that she too was in the same situation. When I spoke about this to my mother saying that Chris had been pregnant so soon my mother said in her usual matter of fact way, 'I am not a bit surprised about the news, as what else is a couple to do stuck in the wilds of Perthshire in January?', and as usual I suppose she was right. It was a bigger surprise about Betty's news after almost eight years of marriage, but we were all delighted for her and Joe. When I told my mother-in-law about the news of the pregnancies and said as usual I was later than the others and was being left behind, she said completely out of the blue, 'Have you ever considered adoption?' I was completely taken by surprise at her question but I answered truthfully that I had never contemplated such an action. Like most people I had taken for granted that when you got married children followed as a matter of course. But when this had not happened in my case I just accepted the fact and got on with my life. When I had mentioned the matter to my mother she always said that I had plenty of time to have a family and if they did not make me laugh they would not give me the reason to make me cry. By this I think she meant that children could be a mixed blessing, bringing their sorrows as well as their joys. We did not mention this matter again and I was quite glad to leave it there, but now that my mother in law had brought up the subject I felt that I had to consider it. I know that she, my mother-in-law, was desperate to have grandchildren so maybe I was being selfish in not considering her feelings.

I did not know anything about the adoption procedure, but she said that there was an agency in Glasgow called St. Francis Children's Society that dealt with the adoption of Catholic children and she would arrange for us to pay a visit to see the children. A date was set and we duly went to visit the home of the unmarried mothers. What followed was a nightmare for me. I did not know what I was supposed to be looking for but eventually I saw a little girl who resembled me in colouring, she was about 9-months old and seemed very bright, with dark hair and big brown eyes, so I decided to chose her. It would take a few weeks for things to happen and to get matters settled but the lady in charge said she would keep in touch and let us know what was going on. However, just a few days later I received a letter which said that when the baby's mother had been told that someone wished to adopt her daughter she had changed her mind and decided to keep the child herself. We went back for a second visit and on this occasion I chose a little boy, 6 months old and again with dark hair and eyes, just like me. The person in charge told me that his mother had been engaged to the boy's father, but the affair had finished when she became pregnant. She could not afford to bring up the child herself and her parents had turned her out of the house when she became pregnant before marriage. Once again we had to wait for a few weeks for things to be settled but unbelievably a short time later there was another letter which informed us that the couple on hearing of the adoption had decided to get married and keep the child. I don't think that this state of affairs happened very often and most adoptions go ahead quite smoothly but I had had enough and decided not to go ahead with this idea as I don't think it was meant to be in my case.

My mother-in-law was very disappointed at the outcome but I had tried to please her and it had not worked out, so if it was ordained that I should remain childless then so be it. I really don't think my heart had been in it from the start and I know my mother had been less enthusiastic about this idea of adoption, but as I said I had tried and no one could ask for anymore. I haven't mentioned John in all this, the reason being he had sided with his mother from the outset but if we had adopted a child it would have been left to me to bear the brunt of rearing the child and it would not have involved him as much. I know that he was too easily influenced by his mother and that what she said was law, but I had a mind of my own and I did not intend to be coerced into anything against my better judgement, no matter how well meaning the other person might be. I admired my mother-in-law for all her good qualities, of which she had many, but I did not intend to be moulded into the person she wanted me to be. With all my imperfections I was my own person and intended to remain so whether it pleased others or not, unlike like John who took the line of least resistance, especially where his mother was concerned.

Chris and David had a baby boy, born at the end of September 1950, a bonny fair haired child and Chris asked me if I would like to be his Godmother. Of course I agreed immediately and considered it an honour to accept. I don't think my Aunt Mary was very pleased, as at that time it was usual for the person who had best maid or bridesmaid to be Godmother to the first child of the marriage, but Chris stuck to her decisions. She only had my cousin Betty as her bridesmaid because of my Aunt Mary who has been so persistent about it, but she felt that she had the right to decide who would be the Godmother to her child, so my Aunt Mary got no say in the matter. To make things even better, Father Joe agreed to Christen the baby, his first baptism since his ordination. So the baby was duly baptised and named Brian, not a family name but one that Chris and David liked. Usually the first boy was named after the father or the grandfather, but that custom was slowly dying out and parents were now choosing names that they preferred and not upholding the old traditions. Joe and Betty however decided to name their first child Charlotte in honour of Betty's mother. Their second child, also a girl, was called Rose after my mother, and their third child, a boy, Joe for his father and his grandfather, my father. So they had stuck to the old ways of doing things.

Brian was a lovely little boy and I used to enjoy taking him with me anywhere I went to show him off. I bought him his first set of clothes, a little jacket and long trousers. It was a brown tweed suit and he looked so handsome in it, with his lovely fair hair and his sturdy little body.

David was now working in the Civil Service in a lowly position but with great chances of advancement. His wages were not very large but they had a little house in Springburn with a very low rent so they managed quite well. David was paid monthly so Chris had four small purses and put a weekly amount in each of the purses so she did not get into any debt before the end of the month. She was young in years, just over 20, but she had an old head on her young shoulders. She was also very good with her hands, for example at knitting and sewing, and made all Brian's outfits herself, so he was always well dressed. In later years, although she was very comfortably placed financially, she never lost her canny streak and would not spend money on something that she could make herself.

My older sister Annie was cast in the same mould, very efficient and always prepared for any emergency. She was also clever with her hands in all the womanly pursuits, like knitting, sewing and dressmaking, but I think the mould must have been lost when it came to me. I did not have any desire to learn these womanly arts. Both of my sisters could follow an intricate knitting pattern and watch television at the same time. I could just about manage to knit a scarf with just rows of plain and purl stitches.

As a case in point, a few years previously my mother had bought a new Singer sewing machine, and with it came a small bonus of 12 free dressmaking lessons by Singers. My mother thought it would be a good chance for me to learn how to make my own clothes, but once again I was a big disappointment to her; I preferred to go dancing rather than sit over a boring sewing machine. So my mother lost the bonus lessons and I was in her bad books again. As they say, no two people in the one family are alike and in my case this was certainly true, as my sister and I were poles apart. Even my mother used to say that if she had not known differently she would swear that I had been adopted. I knew that I was good at counting rows of figures and my teachers always said I was good at composition, but I suppose these assets were not the requirements needed to run a household and to keep children fed and clothed. I kept telling myself that maybe as I got older I would change and become more responsible but I knew in my heart that this would never happen. My main trouble was that I had a very low boredom threshold and when I was bored with anything I just gave up and moved onto something more interesting, with the result that the boring thing never got finished and nothing was accomplished. Well at least that is my excuse, and I am sticking to it.

Speaking of boring things and as an example, I once tried to turn a collar on a shirt. After unpicking the stitches on the worn side, I turned it around and stitched it up again only to discover when I was finished that I had the button hole on the same side as the button. So what could I do? If it had been my sisters, they would have made a new buttonhole on the other side, but I knew that I could not do this. So I went out and bought a new shirt.

And speaking of how efficient my sisters were, when Chris was expecting her first child, her case with all the baby clothes, napkins, safety pins, shawl etc. were all prepared weeks before the due date of birth. The case stood at the bottom of her bed ready for the big day and she even left coppers for the phone if David had to phone the hospital when the birth was imminent. That was something that would never have occurred to me, but then that was the difference between us. When we were in The Guide movement, our motto was 'Be Prepared', but that was one Guide promise I never carried out. It was standing joke in our family that I would be late even for my own funeral. I never really understood this because if you were dead you would not be moving or going anywhere, just lying there waiting for someone to take you away. So I even I with my record could not be late for that.

I have not said much about my brother Peter, the youngest of the boys and the one nearest to me in age and personality. He was different from John and Joe as they were taller and more sturdily built. Peter was not very tall, was very pale in complexion with rather fine features, and was very neat and fussy about his appearance. My mother said that he had been a very delicate baby and unlike the rest of us very slow at learning to walk, as he was almost three years of age before he was completely steady on his feet and able to run around. She said that the rest of us could walk long before our first birthday but Peter had a lack of calcium in his bones so it took him longer, though once he started he soon made up for lost time. We were quite close in age, only two years between us, and at that time he was my favourite brother. As I said before, we all had our party piece, which we would sing at family gatherings. Peter and I used to harmonise a song called 'Souvenirs', and the last two lines were, 'I count them all apart and when the tear drops start, I find a broken heart among my souvenirs'. At this point we would pretend to sob bitterly on one another's shoulder. It always raised a laugh with the family and we also enjoyed it.

John would sing an Irish song, naturally, which had five or six verses and seemed to go on forever. It was called 'Three Bonnie Lassies from Banyon' and it ended up, 'And I am the best of them all'. I don't know where he dug it up from as I had never heard it before or since, but it would have been kinder to have left it buried and rested in peace. I don't mean to be cruel to John but he was so different from the rest of us and I just could not understand him. It was many years later before I could see and appreciate all his good qualities. Peter had a very kind nature and was very thoughtful especially with regard to my mother, and a few years later, when she was 70 years of age, he saved up 70 brand-new half crowns and gave them to her for her birthday. That was quite a lot of money to receive in those days as a birthday present but it was the thought that had gone into the gift, and not the money, that gave my mother the most pleasure. As I mentioned before, Joe my oldest brother was a very handsome person. He was quite tall and had a nice build. There was a well-know shop in Glasgow called 'Burton's, the 50 Shillings Tailors' where you could buy a very decent suit for that price, the equivalent of about £2.50 in today's money. Joe used to buy all his suits there and the manager always said that he had the perfect Burton figure. I believe that this name is still popular in the High street today but I don't think the price will be the same as it was then.

Speaking of High Street stores, things there were changing very quickly. In most of the large shops there were now restaurants where you could have tea or coffee while shopping, or lunch if you preferred it at a very reasonable price. Before the war most people never dined out except for weddings or funerals but during the war when rationing was so tight, a chain of shops was opened which were called British Restaurants. You could have quite a decent meal there for a shilling. Nothing fancy of course, but a plate of mince or potatoes, or stew with vegetables, and this was a godsend when food was in short supply. These eating-places soon became very popular and people soon got used to dining out. Shopping now had become more of a pleasure than a dull chore as one could meander round the stores and then relax in the warmth of the cosy environment of the restaurant and have a snack or a meal and a chance to rest your tired feet.

My mother loved to get out of the house for a few hours as she was on her own all day when the boys were at work. So I used to take her shopping once or twice a month and she really looked forward to these outings. On one of these shopping trips we had gone to 'Dallas', one of our favourite shops in town. She was going to an outing with the Co-op girls the following week and as it was quite near to her birthday I had decided to treat her to a new outfit and a birthday lunch for the event. We went to the coat department and she saw a coat that she liked but when she tried it on I thought that it looked a bit on the loose side but the assistant said, 'You look lovely in that Madam, and it is a perfect fit'. But I noticed that she was holding about a yard of extra material in her hand at my mother's back to make it look as though it fitted, so I just said, 'No thanks, we will look at something else that is more fitting'. She did not look too pleased at losing the sale but I was not as green as maybe I looked, and working in a shop I knew all the tricks of the trade. So we looked for something else. My mother did not know why I was making a fuss and said,

'I liked that coat'. But of course she could not see what was going on behind her back. We eventually found another coat and a nice print dress to go with it. Then it was onto the hat department as my mother never went anywhere without a hat. My mother used to always wear black or navy colours as her head gear, but I had noticed a lovely dusky pink hat which I knew would suit her. She kept saying, 'I am far too old to wear that colour', but I insisted that she try it on. As I said before, my mother had a lovely complexion and I knew this colour would look good on her, and eventually when she tried it on and looked in the mirror she agreed with me, so I bought the hat. We then went to the cash desk to pay for our purchases but the excitement was not over yet. The girl on the cash desk was very young and seemed to be a bit inexperienced; three times she counted the total of the purchases and three times she arrived at different amounts. My mother by this time was losing patience and eventually she said to the girl, 'My lassie also works as a cashier, so why don't you let her count it for you and let us get out of here and go home?'. I told my mother that the girl was not allowed to do this but by this time the girl too was becoming very flustered, so I agreed to count it for her and told her to put the amount in her own writing on the slip. I paid it and got out of the store as quickly as we could before any more mishaps occurred. It was a memorable shopping day, but at least my mother looked lovely in her new outfit, so all was well that ended well. Things were never dull when my mother was around, but I would not have changed her for the world.

When I lived in Down Street there was a lady who lived at the bottom of the street, her name was Ina and we used to meet quite often when we went shopping in the little general store. Her husband was a long distance train driver and was away from home quite a lot, and as she had no family of her own she got quite lonely sometimes. My half-day off was on a Tuesday, so I invited her to come to tea on those afternoons. It was a break for her and a bit of company for me also. After a few of these visits she asked me if I would like her to read my tea leaves to see what my future had in store. I did not believe in fortune telling of any kind and thought it was a bit of hocus pocus, but I as I did not want to hurt her feelings I agreed. She looked into my cup and told me all the usual things that were generally said on these occasions: I would never be rich, but I would always have enough to get by on; I would have a long life and a happy one etc, etc. I listened and nodded my head but did not believe a word of it. But I guess it was a bit of harmless fun and she believed in what she was saying so why make a big fuss about it, although why anyone should imagine that your future could be seen in a few leaves at the bottom of a cup was beyond me.

On one of these visits my brother-in-law Jimmy was also there visiting me and after a cup of tea Ina again offered to read the tea leaves. I told her to read Jimmy's cup instead of my cup as she had done mine just the week previously, so Jimmy passed over his cup to her and after spending a few minutes studying the contents she looked up at Jimmy and said you will be changing your job in a three, which is either three weeks or three months, and moving to a new house round about the same time. Jimmy started laughing and said, 'I don't know about moving house, but I definitely won't be changing my job'. As I have mentioned before, Jimmy worked in Blochairn steel works and had been in the same job for years and also he loved his job, but Ina was quite adamant that this was going to happen. I left them both still arguing about it and as usual I took it all with a pinch of salt and thinking it all a load of rubbish. But strange to say, in three months time Blochairn steel works had closed and all its workers were made redundant, and a few weeks later Jimmy and Annie received a letter from the Glasgow Corporation housing department informing them that they had been allocated a new flat in a newly built block of houses in their area.

I am sitting on the fence on this one as I don't know what to believe. Could it be true that anyone could see the future in a few tea leaves? Or was it just an extraordinary stroke of luck that Ina had guessed accurately what was going to happen in the future? She had told me once before about an incident that had happened to her about a woman who had come to see her and who asked her to read her cup. This had happened during the war and the woman had received word that her husband had been reported missing believed dead, and having heard no more word in the next two years had as a last resort come to Ina to see if she could tell her anything more. Ina had read the leaves and told her that her husband was alive, she could see the man sitting with other men in an enclosure surrounded by a wire fence. When the war was over the woman had come to visit Ina to thank her and to bring her a present. She had just got word that her husband was on his way home after three years in a prisoner of war camp. When Ina had told me this story I had just put it down to a lucky guess on her part, but now I was not so sure of anything anymore. As the saying goes stranger things happen in the universe than are ever dreamed of in philosophy. So could it be true that some people truly had the gift of second sight and could foretell the future, and I had the good fortune to know one? I realised now that I should never scoff at things that are beyond my understanding.

Chapter 12

I was now working in a grocery store in Port Dundas, a few miles away from my home. This establishment was owned by two brothers, Abraham and Edward Vaughn. They also owned the dairy next door. Abi, as the older brother liked to be known, was quite a distinguished looking man, with white hair and very fair skin. Eddie his brother was a lot younger and had a darker skin and black curly hair, and he was very much the subordinate of the two in every way. I had seen the advertisement for this job in the local paper and I had written in and asked for an interview, stating my experience of shop work. I received a reply in a few days and was asked to come to the shop and told to enquire for Mr Vaughn, who was to give me the interview. When I arrived at the address I had been given I discovered that there were two shops together with the same name above the door, so I went into the first one and asked the assistant if I could have a word with the manager. I had dressed very smartly for the occasion, in a new raincoat and matching hat, and the assistant was very deferential in manner and said, 'If you would like to wait for a minute Madam, I shall inform Mr Vaughn that you are here'. I thought to myself, 'What a charming girl, and so polite'. Mr Vaughn came in and when I said that I had come about the vacancy he looked quite taken aback but took me into the office and asked me about my previous jobs etc. After a few other questions he told me that I could start in the grocery shop next door on the following Monday. I found out later why I received such a polite welcome and why he had been so surprised to see me. At that time parents with a child under five and below average income were given tokens for free milk for the child. These tokens came in a green book and could only be used for that child and no one else. The shop had to keep a record of all these people who were entitled to claim the benefit and periodically an inspector called to check their records and to ensure that they were only getting free milk for the holders of the green book and for no one else. In other words they were not 'milking' the system. When I had shown up in all my finery, they had mistaken me for the milk inspector, and supposedly had passed this information onto Mr Vaughn who then found out that it was only me applying for a job of a lowly shop assistant. Well they do say that clothes maketh the man, so I suppose that applies to women as well.

The grocers was a very busy shop and situated in a prime position in the middle of a housing scheme. There were four assistants and if we were extra busy Eddie would always lend a hand, and even Abi helped out when required. One of the assistants was called Janette Thompson and she was quite a character. She just opened her mouth and said what she thought, whether it was complimentary or not. But she was a very hard worker and well liked by the staff and the customers. She was in charge of the vegetable department and one day when the bags of potatoes were delivered she had been busy with a customer and had not had time to move them from where the delivery man had left them. The boss noticed them lying and asked her to move them as they were a danger to the customers. These bags weighed about a hundredweight each, and were usually put into place by delivery men, so Janette said to the boss, 'My name is Thampson, not Samson'. We all expected Abi to give her a telling off for being so impudent, but like the rest of us he could not stop laughing and, knowing Janette, took it in good part.

On Mondays we used to make up the sugar for the week. These came in large sacks which weighed about the same as the potatoes and it took about four of us all day Monday and half day Tuesday to finish the job. We worked as a team. One filled the bags, one weighed them, one parcelled up the sugar, and the fourth packed them away in the crate provided. On the other days we did the same job with the butter, lard, cheese and dried fruits, and also pulses like barley and lentils. In those days nothing came pre-packed; even the cheese came in a big cask and it had to be cut by wire into requested lengths. We all used to hate this, as the cheese had a skin all round it which had to be scraped off before we could wire it. Another job we all hated was the lard. We made an awful mess of our hands, but Abi would say, 'I don't know what you are moaning about, it is saving you the price of hand cream and keeps your skin nice and supple'.

Abi was a hard taskmaster, but if you worked hard and did your job properly he was quite a decent boss. He employed his own personal accountant who worked in his office for most of the week. When I had been in the job for a few weeks and had become quite friendly with her, she told me that he had made most of his money during the war years and he was now a very wealthy man. But to be fair to him he had worked hard to get where he was and deserved his rewards. I got on quite well with him but I used to get so embarrassed about the way he spoke and acted towards Eddie. He was always making rude remarks and taking him down, but Eddie never retaliated, I used to squirm with embarrassment for him. As I said, Abi was definitely the dominant partner and Eddie was treated like the hired help.

In those days the customer's order was written down on a piece of paper with the price of the item beside it and totalled up at the bottom by the assistant. There were no electric registers in those days. Every now and again Abi would make a spot check to see if your prices were correct and your sum total also. Prices of goods had to be learned; as I said, there was nothing pre-priced when they arrived at the shop. On one of the occasions when Abi was doing his check he stopped at the girl standing next to me on the counter and asked to see her list. He picked up one bag which she had marked down as six chocolate biscuits but when he opened the bag it contained six packets of cigarettes. It turned out that the customer was a friend of the girl assistant and this friend was getting the cigarettes at the price of the biscuits. The assistant was sacked on the spot, of course, and it was a cursory lesson to the rest of us that it did not pay to try and pull the wool over Abi's eyes. He knew all the tricks of the trade. I don't think anyone in the shop tried that trick again. I remained working at this shop for almost seven years and eventually ended up as manageress, but that's another story.

In December of 1952, David, Chris's husband, got a posting to Canonbie, not far from Carlisle. When they had time to settle in a new home, my mother and I decided to pay them a visit. They lived in a little hamlet called Rowanburn which consisted of one small general store and one public house called The Cross Keys. On the day we arrived we knocked at the door but did not get any answer, but we could hear voices and the noise of someone digging at the back of the house. We walked round to the rear of the building and there was my usually-ladylike young sister dressed in a pair of old wellington boots and an old jacket digging up the ground, and Brian the baby sitting happily beside her. It was such a total surprise to me that my young sister who was a complete novice to hard labour was digging away at the ground like an Irish navvie. My mother and I just looked at one another in amazement and I could just imagine my mother thinking to herself, 'This is why I paid out good money for my daughters education, to see her reduced to this?'. However, we did not have to worry about Chris; she was entirely happy with her new life, she had marvellous neighbours who kept an eye on her and the baby, and she loved village life where everyone knew one another and looked after each other.

When the lady next door was baking she would hand in some of her scones or cakes for David and Chris and Brian to enjoy. There was a woollen mill in the town and one of the ladies who worked there handed in a bail of material to Chris so she could make up some clothing for her or Brian on her sewing machine. When we left to go home my mother and I, instead of feeling sorry for her, really envied her for the quiet peaceful life she was enjoying in that little village. She told us that when she took Brian out in his pram she could walk for miles through the country lanes without meeting anyone at all, only seeing fields of sheep or cows, but she never felt nervous or alone as it was such a peaceful place. And of course the open spaces and good country air was such a healthy environment for Brian to grow and to thrive. She stayed there for quite a few years and loved every minute of her country life.

Meanwhile at home my father-in-law took ill and had to go into hospital for a few weeks. I used to wonder what he and my mother-in-law talked about when she went to visit as I had never heard them having a conversation about anything in the years that I had been part of the family. They were very polite to one another but there was no common ground between them, or any kind of warmth.

I could sympathise with both of them, as my own marriage was anything but ideal. We too were exact opposites of one another. We had no rows or arguments but no closeness either. John was, or seemed to be, quite happy just to take each day as it came, but I felt that there must be more to life than this dull routine that our marriage had become, with each day the same as the day before, no excitement and nothing to look forward to but more of the same. I was only in my late twenties but sometimes I felt middle-aged long before my time. I was on my own every night from the time that John went to work, except for the occasional visit from Nora or one of my family. I had too much time to sit and brood and wonder why my life had become so grey, and my marriage so dull and meaningless. I know that lots of people have much worse lives than I had. John was a good worker and provider, he did not drink or abuse me in any way, and we had enough to live on and I did not go short of anything, but it was not what I wanted from life or marriage. But what was the answer to my problem? People like us did not break up a marriage because they were bored or unhappy, and in our circles divorce was entirely out of the question, and in any case I had no grounds for such an option. I could not admit that my marriage was a failure because I wanted more excitement in my life than I was getting, and I didn't think I would get much of a sympathetic hearing. I would probably be told to count my blessings instead of feeling sorry for myself.

I know now that my early basic instincts that we were not suitable as a couple had been right, and if only John had not taken ill with malaria that night when I had decided that it would not work out between us, it would have been all over between us at that time. I suppose life is made up with, 'if only I had done this or that, life would have been changed'. If only I had not been influenced by other people into thinking I was making a good match and marrying into a good decent family and had not got carried away with the excitement of getting engaged and then rushing into marriage when I knew I was not really ready for such a large commitment, my life would have taken a different path. But I had got married and no one had forced me into it, I had taken a solemn vow in church on my wedding day and I had to adhere to that now. There was no going back on that and even if my life was not as perfect as I would have wished, that was something I would just have to learn to live with and could do nothing about. At least during the day I had my work and that helped to take my mind off my personal problems. But at night I would lie in bed and all my worries and doubts would come crowding in again. I would think of my parents-in-law and the half-life that they shared, and I wondered if history was repeating itself and that we were going down the same path that they had trod. If only there had been someone I could confide in and ask for their advice but there was nobody that I felt would understand or appreciate my feelings of utter loss of direction my life was taking. So I guessed there was no answer to my problems and this was just something that I had to live with, and make the best of, and get on with my life as best as I could manage.

My young sister told me years later that she had remarked to my mother that she always seemed to make more allowances for me than she did for the rest of the family, and my mother had replied that if she had it was only because she knew I was very unhappy. If only I had known that then I could have confided in her and things might have turned out differently. I had never complained to my mother about my marriage, but I guess mothers know these things instinctively where their families are concerned.

At this time in Glasgow there was a lot of building work taking place. The old tenements were being knocked down and the tenants were being sent to the new housing estates on the outskirts of Glasgow. These new houses were mostly semi-detached and with a garden at the rear of the house. They were fresh and modern but with no feeling of closeness or warmth that the old tenements had contained. Most of them were more or less concrete jungles and were miles away from shops and other amenities that Glasgow had always taken for granted. There was no popping in or out of each other's houses or having a gossip on the landings. Everyone had their own front door and most of them remained behind it. My mother was a little more fortunate than most; she had been allocated a house in the Milton district which was a smaller complex and not too distant from the neighbourhood in which we had lived before. She really did not want to move at all; she had been happy where she was, but one by one her neighbours were moving away and she was living with strangers, and as quite a few of them were going to her allocated area she decided that she would move there also. The new house was nice with a large lounge and the bedrooms upstairs, and a pleasant back garden. There was a feeling of the countryside as there were lots of green fields around and a small farm at the end of the street. She was living next door to a family of a husband and wife and two daughters. The couple Jean and Sam had also had Jean's widowed mother staying with them, and the mother was closer to my mother in age. They were very friendly people, so my mother was very fortunate in that respect. I don't think she ever felt really content there, or really settled into her new home. She missed the companionship of people she had known for years and who were more like family than just neighbours. It was very pleasant in the summer when she could sit in the garden admiring the flowers and watching the birds, of which she was very fond. But in the winter it was not as warm or cosy as the old house. I suppose the fact that the house was new and had not been weathered with the sun over the years would make a big difference. The one good point in our favour was that I could call every lunch time as the bus stop was only a few minutes from our shop and I was dropped off at the top of the street where my mother lived. So it broke up the day for her and gave me a chance to pick up all the family gossip, and of course it was very nice for me to come home for a nice hot lunch.

The boys were still with my mother. I don't think they had any intention of settling down or maybe it was they knew that they would not be so well looked after anywhere else. My mother waited on them hand and foot. Peter had a few lady friends over the years but nothing very serious, and John seemed settled into bachelorhood. Of course they were company for my mother and I would not have liked to think that she was on her own as this would have been a cause for concern for the rest of the family. But then again, she was getting on in years and still doing all her own housework, cooking and washing for the boys, and never complaining. I guess that she was just glad that she was able enough to do as she had always done, looking after the family and their needs.

As I had said before I had took her out when I could and gave her little treats and I know she looked forward to these outings. But with me now working full time these events did not happen as often as I would have liked. I know she understood my position and realised that work had to come first.

My sister Annie and her husband Jimmy used to take her to the pictures on a Saturday evening, but as much as she enjoyed this she told me that Jimmy used to fall asleep half way through the film and she missed most of it because he was snoring so loudly. So I guess it was a bit of a mixed blessing for her, but at least they did try to help out.

David, Chris's husband was moving slowly up the promotion ladder and in 1955 received notice that he was being sent to Mönchengladbach in Germany. The only problem was that there were no family quarters for the family. So Chris had to remain at home until accommodation was found for them. She stayed with my older sister Annie for a time but it was not an ideal situation, with Annie's three children in the house as well. So after a time she asked if she could come and stay with me until she could join David in Germany. I agreed to this of course, and told her I would be glad of the company. She stayed with me for a short time and later she went to London to wait there for their departure date. She said that this was the loneliest time of her life. She was staying in rented accommodation and, now with two small children, it was not an ideal situation. She knew nowhere there and found that the people were very cold and distant and not like the kinder more warm-hearted Glaswegians. She wrote to David telling him how lonely and unhappy she was feeling and eventually he managed to acquire hotel accommodation for her and the children in Mönchengladbach. She really enjoyed staying in the hotel as everything was done for them; maids to clean the room, and meals served in the premises. She was living a life of luxury and enjoying every moment of it. The children loved it too as they were getting utterly spoiled by everyone, and enjoyed all the attention. Eventually they were allocated a house and settled down to their new life in Germany. Chris loved her time there as there were plenty of shops and a good social life, in sharp contrast to what had gone before. She even had a maid, Helga, to help with the household duties.

After a time, my mother, John and I decided to visit her. We went by boat via the Hook of Holland where David met us, and then by train to Germany. When we were on the train the customs men to came to check our passports. When they came to my mother there was a lot of conversation between them and much pointing of fingers in my mother's direction. She was getting quite upset as she thought something was wrong with her passport. When one of them started to smile and speak to her she became quite flustered and asked David who understood German what the man was saying, David began to laugh and said that he was wishing her a happy birthday, which had happened a few days previously. They had noticed her birth date on the passport and were only wishing a belated happy birthday. What a relief that was.

We had a lovely holiday, but my mother never got used to the idea of Chris having a maid, and when we were having a cup of tea or something to eat she would say to Chris, 'Aren't you going to give the girl something to eat?'. Chris had to explain that the girl was not one of the family and had her break at different times, but my mother just could not understand this and continued to feel sorry for 'that poor girl', as she called her. I guess my mother was not meant to have a life as one of the leisured classes. As I said before we had a lovely holiday, but something happened on our way home that spoiled things for us. While we were in Germany, John my brother had borrowed Chris's camera to take a few pictures of some of the places we had seen and took the roll of film with him to get developed when he got home. When we arrived at Rotterdam on our way back we were stopped at the customs and they found the roll of film in John's luggage. They insisted that John must have a camera which he was concealing and when he tried to explain that he had borrowed his sister's camera to take the photographs they would not believe him and took him to another room for a strip search. My mother and I were in a terrible state; we were in a strange country, we did not know the language, and we did not know what was happening to John. After a few hours they eventually released him. They had not found a camera of course, and eventually they had to admit defeat. But this incident spoiled our holiday and my mother did not settle down for the rest of the journey home.

At the end of the following year, 1956, my mother-in-law became ill with flu symptoms which after a short time developed in pneumonia, and shortly afterwards she died. John, of course, was dreadfully upset and as I uttered the banal words of comfort that one uses at times like this, I knew that these words meant nothing to him in his hour of grief. He had lost his mother and best friend and I don't think he ever recovered from his loss. Father Joe had his religion to sustain him. He had given his mother the last rites of the Church and was proud to be able to do so, but John did not have this to sustain him and my heart bled for his loss. I had only words to give him and these are so empty when tragedy befalls you. It was the first break in his family and knowing how I had felt when my father had passed away, I could feel his pain. My mother-in-law was a good woman and had deserved to have a good life, but her only real happiness was found in her career of teaching children. At least she had some satisfaction with this, but her personal life was not very fulfilling, and I felt very sorry for her and for all those wasted years which could have been so much happier for her than they were.

When Chris had gone to Germany she was two-and-a-half months pregnant. A few months later her baby was born, another boy who they named Peter, after my young brother. But their joy was short lived. Peter was born with spina bifida. I believe it is a condition where the bones of the spine have not fused together and most babies with this condition don't live for more than a few months. Chris was heartbroken and blamed herself for something she had maybe done or not done when she was pregnant. However, the doctor told her that this condition happened at the moment of conception, and no one was to blame. It was just one of these tragedies that can happen to anyone. If the baby lived managed to live until he was six months old they would have tried to operate to put things right, but unfortunately Peter died at two months old. He was buried in a plot in a military section of Cologne Cathedral reserved for officers and their families. Chris and David were utterly bereft. At home my mother was heartbroken at the news. Chris was the youngest of our family and her baby, and now in her hour of need we were separated by hundreds of miles and my mother was unable to give her any comfort or consolation. But she was determined to go to Germany as soon as possible to be with her.

When we finally made that journey about a year later, one night when Chris and I were on our own in the lounge with a cup of coffee, I noticed a photograph on the mantle piece which I did not recognise. I asked Chris if the baby in the picture was Peter and she nodded. I said how sorry I was for her loss, and she suddenly burst into floods of tears. I apologised for bringing up the subject when it was still so painful for her, but she said she was glad I had done so, as when she came home from hospital after Peter's death nobody ever mentioned his name and it was as though he never existed. She knew that this was to spare her feelings, but she said she had needed to talk about him; he was her baby and in his short life she had loved and nursed him and did not want him to be forgotten. She needed to mourn for him and while everyone avoided the subject, she was not given the chance to do so. Her grief had to have an outlet and now it was happening. He would always be a part of her family and she would never forget him, and she did not want others to forget him either. I shed a few tears myself that night, but at least for her the dam had finally broken and now she might be able to move forward.

On a less sombre note on the television at that time there was lots of discussions about space travel and in 1957 the USSR launched the first man made satellite, Sputnik One, which was followed by Sputnik Two, with the dog Laika on board. It was said that in the course of a few years a man would land on the moon. This was indeed a mind-blowing thought, but on the home front something equally earth shattering was happening. My brother John, the self confessed, confirmed, bachelor had started courting. Her name was Marie and she was Italian. She and her sister Selistina had come to work in Glasgow in the laundry of the eye hospital where John was employed in the boiler room. Marie and her sister came from a small village near Venice named Montebello where work was scarce and there was a lot of poverty after the war. So they had come to this country to try and find jobs so that they could send back some money to help their family at home. Marie could not speak English and John only had a few words of Italian, but as resourceful as ever he had bought an English-Italian phrase book and this was how the courtship progressed. Trust our John to be different from the usual run-of-the mill majority!

Cupid was pointing his bow in other directions also. My niece Rose, my Sister Annie's daughter, was also in a steady relationship and they were saving to get married in the near future. She had asked me if I would be her matron of honour at her wedding which I thought was a lovely compliment and I had agreed immediately. Rose and I had become quite close. She stayed with me a few times at the weekend and if she had any problems she would ask for my advice in solving them. There was only eleven years between us in age and there were some things that were a bit embarrassing for her to talk to her parents about, and that needed to be discussed with an impartial observer and I filled that bill. Rose was married the following year and was a lovely white bride and I was in a lilac taffeta dress. It was a perfect day and everyone had a great time on the occasion. Her baby was born the following year, a daughter called after her mother, and her mother's mother. So there was another Rose in the family.

John and Marie were married in the following January in 1957 and went on to have four children, two boys and two girls, in their married life. John took care of all the mundane things of life; he did all the shopping and paid all the bills until such times that Marie became familiar in handling our money. She was about fifteen years younger than John, who was 35 years old at that time, but she soon learned about our ways and settled down to married life. I was full of admiration about John and his patience and understanding he showed with her, and I saw another side of my brother that I had never suspected was there.

It was a happy time for my family but as usually happened in life, the happy times did not last forever and already there were dark clouds looming behind the blue skies. When Rose's baby was born she wanted to have a photograph taken over the four generations: the baby, herself, my sister Annie and my mother. On the appointed day I was at my mother's house as usual for lunch and when she was getting ready to meet Rose and Annie I suggested that I should apply a little make up on her face to tone down the shine of her skin which would produce a better photograph. My mother was very dubious about this as she had never used make up before, but when I promised that it would only be a little cream, powder and lip stick she finally agreed. When I had finished my mother looked really nice and even she agreed with me that it was a big improvement and seemed quite proud of herself and her new appearance. I walked with her to the bus stop where she was catching the bus into town to meet Annie and Rose. While we were standing at the bus stop, one of the neighbours came up and started to chat with my mother. She looked at her and then did a double take and said, 'You look very well Mrs Dawson, but there is something different about you'. My mother laughed and said, 'Oh, that's because this daughter of mine's put some make up on my face'. Her friend replied, 'Oh, I could not be bothered with all that carry on. I am quite happy with what God gave me'. My poor mother, who had never had make up on before and now must have felt like a fallen woman.

The next day when I went to their house I asked how things had gone at the photographers, my mother said everything had gone very well and then she added that when the photographers were putting people in the group in the right order he had looked first at my mother, then Annie, and said, 'Which one is the Great grandmother?'. Of course, my mother was very flattered by his remark and said to me in all seriousness, 'Of course, our Annie has put on an awful lot of weight recently and that makes you look older'. I laughed inwardly as I looked at her less-than-Twiggy-like figure and conceded that she had a valid point, but in my thoughts I said to myself, 'What a little make up will do for your confidence'.

The only down side of that day was that my mother had caught a chill while standing waiting for her bus home. There was a cold biting wind blowing and there was no shelter at the bus stop. She said she still felt a bit shivery and could not seem to get warm even after she had arrived home. I told her to go to bed with a hot water bottle, but she shrugged this off and said she would be alright in a day or two. Knowing how determined she was I did not pursue the matter. The next day however, she was still not feeling very well and there was a slight yellow tinge on her face that I had not seen before so we decided to call the doctor to see her. When he came and examined her he thought that it might be a touch of jaundice or a slight liver complaint and decided to send her to the hospital for tests. This was a big shock to the family. My mother had never been ill and the last time she had been forced to lie in her bed was when she had pleurisy quite a few years before. But we did not want to take any chances with her health, especially at her age, so we agreed with the doctor that the hospital would be the best place for her, as she would be looked after properly. I wrote to Chris in Germany and told her what had happened and she said that she would come home immediately. I explained that she was only going into hospital for tests and that there was no immediate cause for concern and to wait until we had the results before she decided to travel, and eventually she agreed to do so.

My mother was in the hospital for a few weeks but the doctors still could not find out what was wrong with her. The family visited every night and she seemed fine, always quite chatty and cheerful but longing to get home again. In the meantime, Marie and John had had their first baby who they named Anna Marie. Marie brought the baby up to visit my mother and after holding her and saying what I lovely baby she was she said something very strange. When they were leaving she kissed the baby and said, 'I am so sorry but I won't be seeing you again'. Marie said, 'Of course you will, I will bring her up when I come to visit you'. But my mother just smiled and shook her head. A few nights later, when Annie and I were visiting the hospital my mother seemed as cheerful as usual ,and I said to Annie how well she seemed and that I did not think she would be in the hospital for very much longer. Annie looked a bit doubtful and said that yes, she seemed a lot better, but hadn't I noticed something a bit strange that had happened that evening? I said that I had not noticed anything unusual and she said, 'Did you not see when she took a drink from that bottle on her bedside table?'. My mother had never been able to drink from a bottle; she always said that she felt she would choke when she tried, and oddly enough I have the same problem, I dismissed her worries at the time, but this incident worried me later when I thought about it. My mother took a turn for the worse in the early hours of the following morning and died. When they sent word to Peter and he spoke to the Doctor in charge of my mother's case, even he could not explain what had happened. He said that her heart was as sound as bell and he could find no reason why she had gone so suddenly, or without any warning. She was seventy two years of age.

The family were devastated. The heart of our family had stopped beating and we were left in despair. It was left to me to break the news to Chris and she was really bitter. She said that I had not let her come over when my mother was alive and she wasn't coming that she was dead. It was a cold miserable morning in February 1958 when my mother was laid to rest. She was not put in the family lair as it was already full with my father and the other departed children. But Betty, my sister-in-law, advised us not to open another lair for my mother but to put her in beside Betty's mother who was the only occupant in their family plot. So that is my mother's last resting place. We had abided by my mother's wishes; there had been no wake held. Her body had lain in the Church overnight and then was brought back home to be buried. When I looked at her dead body she looked so peaceful as though she was just sleeping. She even had some colour in her cheeks. I kissed her on the forehead and said my goodbyes and 'rest in peace, dear mother'.

When the cortege left the house, quite a few of our neighbours and friends had gathered, with Nora my friend amongst them. At that time in Glasgow not very many women attended funerals. That was the man's job; the women stayed in the house and did their mourning in private. But that morning when the funeral car piled high with flowers moved away, Nora stepped forward and walked behind. In a few moments all the other women followed suit, and soon there was quite a precession following the hearse. It was a silent tribute to my mother and one which she richly deserved. I had never seen this happen before and when I spoke of it to Nora, who like myself was from Irish descent, she said that this was the usual way they did things in Ireland. That was something I had never known before.

We all have regrets when a loved one dies about things we should have done but did not, or things we had done but should not have. In Chris's case the loss of my mother had not really sunk in properly. She had not been there at the end and did not get the chance to say goodbye. It was a few weeks later when she was shopping in the NAFFI store with a friend in Germany when she said she would have go and get a Mother's Day card, and suddenly Chris realised that never again would she have to buy a card for her mother, and for the first time she realised what she had lost.

In my case, it was something entirely different. My mother did not aspire to be granted very much from life. She was content with what she had and did not wish for anything more but there was one thing that she would have liked to do before she died and that was to visit Blackpool to see the lights. A few years previously I had arranged for her and my Aunt Mary Dawson to go there for the weekend to make her dream come true, but before the planned date my Aunt Mary took ill and could not travel and somehow the chance never came again. Even now after all these years it still hurts that her wish had never been granted. I felt that I could have tried harder to fulfil that wish. The saddest words in our language must be, 'if only'. If only I had done this or had not done that. We know it is already too late to do anything about it, but we are all only too human and we all make mistakes and as they say, we can all be wise after the event.

Chapter 13

In the previous year, my brother Joe's itchy feet had been on the move again and he had gone to England, in a small town called Corby, in the Stuart & Lloyds steel works, where jobs were plentiful and housing was available after a short time of waiting. There was a camp for the workers until such times that they were allocated a council house, but Joe found that the camp was a rather rough place, so he and a friend had decided to share a small caravan situated locally until a house was available. My mother had gone down to visit but was not very happy to see him living in such cramped and damp conditions, as there was no heating in the caravan. But he was determined to stick it out until something better turned up and fortunately it was not long before he was settled in his new home and his family were able to join him there.

We had heard of this town before. In the 1930's my Uncle Tom, my father's younger brother had also gone there to work after his local steel works where he was employed was closed down. It was a very different place then, just a small village with a main street, a few churches, a small cinema and a weekly market. The name Corby was originally due to the Vikings who invaded Britain in the 8th century. They were led by a man called Kori and some of them settled in our area which was known as Koribiekoris which was later to be called Corby.

When the railway was built, there was a great demand for lumber and bricks. So outsiders looking for work had moved in and boosted the village population by large numbers. When the railway was being constructed the building team discovered vast amounts of iron ore in the ground.

In 1880 a Birmingham industrialist called Samuel Lloyd began iron quarrying. In 1910 he began commercial production of iron and an alliance was formed with a tube making firm in 1903 called Stewarts, and so Stewarts and Lloyds was formed.

The firm went from strength to strength and later, when Corby had been chosen in 1932 to be one of the biggest iron and steel and iron complexes in the world, with unlimited prospects for jobs, an invasion of workers poured in which transformed the place from a small village into a modern industrial town. The post-war years saw a great demand for housing and as Corby had been designated a new town, new building was taking place all over the town. With a double assurance of jobs and housing this became the place where people wished to settle and so Corby prospered and grew.

On the home front things were going a bit more smoothly. Since his mother's death John had been like a lost soul, but recently he had joined a Glasgow choir, the Ogilvy Singers, and this helped a lot. He had a very pleasant tenor voice and he seemed to be enjoying the company of the other members of the choir. They met once a week for practice and over the year gave quite a few concerts in community centres and local halls etc., and as these concerts usually took place at the weekend he could fit them in with his work commitments. He had never really had a hobby which took him out of the house and involved him meeting with other people, so I was glad that he found something that he enjoyed doing and at least it gave us something extra to talk about apart from domestic issues, which made a pleasant change.

I also had to find something to do apart from work and domestic chores. I felt sometimes that life was passing me by and I needed something to look forward to apart from the usual humdrum, usual things of everyday life. I had seldom been out socially for months and now I really felt that I needed more excitement in my life.

I had become friendly with another woman recently called Ina Brown. Her sister was a manageress in one of our local shops and Ina worked part time there a few times a week. She was a few years older than me and we began chatting while I was shopping in the store. She was married with two grown up sons and was very lively and outgoing. She was always telling me that she went to old-time dancing once a week and really enjoyed it, as she had become friendly with quite a few people and enjoyed their company. Old-time dancing had become very popular recently and most of the dance halls in the town would hold a session once a week for beginners and more experienced dancers. Ina was always talking about it and had asked me a few times if I would to go with her one night. I had not been to a dance hall in years as John had no interest in that direction, although I always found this surprising as his mother and Father had been very keen dancers when they had been young, and in fact that was how they had met each other. As I had mentioned before, John's father used to play the fiddle at the dances in the local hall, and John's mother had met him on one of these occasions. She was quite musical also and played the piano. Father Joe was a gifted pianist also, but John did not seem to have any leanings in that direction. So maybe being in the choir was a step forward for him.

I thought that I should maybe take up Ina's suggestion and begin dancing again. At least it would give me a taste of social life. I did not see very much of Nora anymore as a few years previously when her parents died her unmarried sister and she had clubbed together to put down a deposit on a bungalow on the outskirts of Glasgow, which they were now sharing. I missed her company and we had been friends for so long and her absence had left a space in my life that so far had not been filled. Maybe now the time had come to bridge that gap, but on second thoughts, maybe me starting to go to dance halls was not the answer. When the sea is calm why cause waves to appear? In any case I didn't really feel much like tripping the light fantastic at the moment, I had been feeling a bit under the weather recently and had had quite a few attacks of nausea and giddiness. Maybe it was something that I had eaten that had upset my stomach, because I had lost my appetite and couldn't face the thought of having to eat, especially in the mornings. These attacks did not last for long and I had found that if I stuck to just having a cup of tea and a plain biscuit for breakfast, I felt alright for the rest of the day.

Joe was settling in very well in Corby. He liked his job and the area. He had a three bedroom house, kitchen and bathroom and a nice little garden. There was a very large percentage of Scots in the town, in fact it was known as Little Scotland. So he felt quite at home there. I intended to go down some weekend in the near future to see them and their new home. There was a bus service from Glasgow called Barton's Buses which took you right into the town centre in Corby, so the journey wouldn't be a problem.

I really envied Joe and Betty having a nice house. There was no chance of us managing to get one on Glasgow for years, if ever, as there was still a waiting list of thousands and we were well down the priority list with us having a two-roomed house and no family. If only we had been able to go to Corby also, I would not have minded waiting a year or so knowing that I would be sure of getting a house eventually. Joe had said they are still building houses there and at this point the time of waiting was a year or two.

I kept dropping hints about this to John, but so far these had been falling on stony ground. The most he would say is that he would think about it and with that I had to be content. If only he had been more ambitious and forward looking, but he seemed quite happy to plod along in the same old way and I was left feeling resentful. So I had decided at the first opportune moment we would have to sit down and have a talk about where we were going. We had been married for almost seventeen years and had made very little progress from where we had started out. There was nothing to keep us here now. My parents had gone and his mother also, and he saw next to nothing of his own father who spent most of his time with Uncle Jimmy, who was now on his own, with his two sons married and in their own homes. Uncle Pat was more or less a recluse since my mother-in-law had died and seldom left his room. The only thing he looked forward to was Father Joe coming every week on his day off to visit. So what was the point of us being there?

I got my chance a few nights later and after we had our meal I told him I wanted to discuss something with him. I made all the points I have already stated and added that I was going to Corby the following weekend and if I liked the place I was intending to put our name down on the housing list. I also said that I did not want him to give me his answer now, but to think it over and let me know what he decided to do. I also stressed that I was determined to get out of the rut we were in and move forward to a better life than we had at present. As I spoke I could see the expression on his face changing, and I knew he was getting angry and ready for an argument. But I had said all I wanted to say and I told him that the decision was up to him to make and as I was going away for the weekend, he had plenty of time to think about it and to let me know his answer. He started to speak, changed his mind, glared at me and walked out of the room. A few minutes later the front door slammed and I knew he had gone to work. Afterwards I started to worry what I had said to him, I had been very blunt and had more or less given him an ultimatum, and nobody likes to be forced into a corner. But the harm, if such, had been done and the words could not be retracted once they had been spoken. The next morning he came home from work and went straight to bed, I guess it would now be the silent treatment until such times he decided to let me know what he was intending to do. I would rather he had argued with me or ranted and raved, but that was not his style. So I would just had to sit it out until he gave me his answer. For the next couple of days there was an uneasy peace between us and the matter was not raised again.

On the following Saturday I left to spend the weekend in Corby. It was lovely to see Joe, Betty and the children again and they made me very welcome. They had a nice house in a nice area, and although there were rows and rows of houses all around there was also a lot of trees and greenery and a wooded area close by, so it was a pleasant change from the Glasgow streets that I was used to. I had phoned home to say that I had arrived alright and that I had liked what I had seen of Corby so far and had asked if it was possible for him to come for a couple of days to see what he thought of it. He was quite non-committal but said he would let me know soon, so with that I had to be content for the moment. The following night he phoned to say that he would be down in a couple of days but he would be going back on the same night as they were very short staffed at work and he could not get any extra time off work. But at least this was better than nothing, and we would be able to sort things out when we were together. I had told Betty and Joe about my plan to put my name down on the housing waiting list and they seemed very pleased about it, so now it all rested with John and his decision. This was around the end of 1960/1961.

John arrived a few days later and when I opened the door and looked at his face my heart sank and I knew it was not going to be plain sailing on his visit. He started complaining about the journey; the bus had had no heating, there had been a couple of breakdowns which had delayed them, and altogether the trip had been a disaster to him and not worth the bother for a one-day visit. He then asked me if I had done anything about the housing situation and when I answered in the negative he said that was just as well as he had no intention of coming to Corby. He had got a job that he liked, his family were close by whereas he had no family in Corby and not much prospect of getting a job in the only trade that he knew - the newspaper business - so why should he bother to change. It was a move that was only for my benefit and not for his and I was being selfish to expect him to fall in with my wishes when there was nothing beneficial in it for him. I was so angry that I was rendered speechless and I suddenly realised that he had never any intention of moving away from Glasgow. He has had stalled on this question for weeks saying he would consider it but I knew now that he had no intention of doing so. He was quite happy to stay in the same old rut and it did not matter what I wanted. I had known that it would not be easy for him to uproot himself but he could have been more honest with me from the start and not kept me hanging on. I also knew that apart from his few years in the Marines he had never worked anywhere else other than the newspaper business since he had left school. He was a stranger to manual work or toiling in a factory, but at least he could have given it a chance. And although, unlike Glasgow, there were only a few newspaper offices in Corby, he would have maybe found something in that line of business, but he had no thought of trying it. We had a real battle of words with each of us calling the other one selfish but by then I knew that I was fighting a losing battle. He had dug his heels in and had no intention of giving ground. His last parting shot to me was to give up this foolish notion and come back home when I had come to my senses. This remark was like a red rag to a bull, and I told him that if I did come back, things would have to change or I would not be back at all. His answer to that was that I could please myself as I always had, and to stop complaining and be thankful for what I had instead of always wanting something more. If I wanted change maybe I could start thinking I could make the change in my way of thinking and consider him and his feelings. Shortly afterwards he left to catch his bus home and left me feeling utterly despondent. The visit had been an absolute disaster and had accomplished nothing. We were as far apart as before.

When Betty and Joe came back I told them what had happened and Joe said that when John had time to think about things he would calm down and get in touch to apologise, but I did not have high hopes in that direction. He was as stubborn as I was once his mind was made up, and he had sounded quite determined in his decision not to move away from home. So if he did not get in touch or would not change his mind where would that leave me? As usual I had spoken first and thought about it afterwards. I had shot the bolt and maybe closed the door for good and was left wondering where did I go from here? When I thought about it afterwards I began to have doubts about myself. Was I too implacable or too selfish and only thought about myself and did not consider his feelings? I was riddled with doubts and anxieties and could not see a way out of the problem and the hole that I had dug myself into. One week passed and one more and there was still no word from him. What had I done, it had never meant to end this way. He had called my bluff and now I was the one who was left waiting and worrying about what was going to happen. When will I ever learn to think first before I speak?

A few days later, I had another bilious attack and I put it down to all the stress and strain I was under, but when Betty heard that I had had a few bouts of this before she insisted that I go and see her doctor and she made the appointment for me. I went to the surgery on the appointed day, still thinking it was a great stuff being made about a stomach upset. The doctor asked me about my symptoms and how long I had been having these attacks, and when I mentioned that they usually happened in the mornings, he called his nurse into the room and began his examination. To my surprise and embarrassment it included an internal one, which I had not been prepared for, and found extremely embarrassing. When he had finished he smiled at me and said: 'Congratulations, you are more than two months pregnant'. After a few questions about my monthly cycles he gave me a probable date of about the 17th of March for the birth. I stood opened mouth and gaped at him, then stupidly said, 'I can't be pregnant, I have been married for 17 years'. At which he laughed and said, 'Well cases like yours do not happen every day, but they are not unusual'. He asked questions about my normal state of health and if I had suffered any serious illnesses. I told him about the scarlet fever I had had when I was eleven years of age, but could not think of any other ailments. When he asked me about my husband's health, I mentioned his bouts of malaria, which now happened very rarely and were never very serious attacks, and these could be controlled by the quinine tablets which had been prescribed. He said that this could explain why I had had such a late pregnancy as malaria could weaken a man and lessen his chances of becoming a father. This was news to me as I had always taken the blame for my inability to conceive, although I had never understood why. My sisters had never had a problem, so why was I the only different one when I was so healthy in every other sense? The doctor then said that I would have to see a doctor regularly to monitor my progress and that I would have to have the birth in a hospital and not at home, as at my age and with a first birth there could be complications. I listened to his words but my mind was elsewhere and was in a daze and full of mixed emotions of joy, fear, and worry about what might lie ahead with my marriage being in the state that it was at present and of what might happen in the future. I had to talk to somebody who would understand my feelings and doubts and so in a mist of fear and uncertainty I slowly walked home to talk to Betty. When she opened the door to me, she looked at my face and said, 'My God, what's the matter? What did the doctor say to upset you?'. At this I promptly burst into tears. She took me into the kitchen and made a cup of tea and when I had calmed down a little and told her what had happened at the surgery she was delighted at the news, as she had thought that with the state I was in the doctor must have told me that I had a serious illness. We sat and talked for a long time and I told her about why I was so worried and upset about what was happening in our marriage and about my worries about what would happen in the future once the baby was born. John and I had never discussed the possibility of having a child since the fiasco of the adoption and as the years passed we just accepted the fact that I was not meant to have any children and that we just had to adjust to that. Now at this time when our situation was at its worst the unexpected had happened. Was it too late now to repair the damage that had been done? Betty let me talk it all out and then said that the baby was the important issue and I had decide what was in the best interest of the child and concentrate on that alone. The trouble was that I did not know what was the right thing to do in that respect. Should I go back in the hope that baby could bring us closer together? And if it did not, what then? I had walked out of my marriage once but leaving a grown man was one thing and leaving a child was something I could never do. I thought of my in-laws and the way their life had been lived. Having a family for them had not made any difference and I did not want that for my child. I needed to give it a happy, settled home life and at this moment my circumstances were in that sense very far from ideal. The only thing that I was certain of was that I wanted this child, but would it be fair to the child to expect it to mend the cracks in my marriage? If only I could foresee the future the answer would be so simple but this was the present and I had to make my decision now, and I just did not know what to do for the best. I could not go on like this any longer and it was not fair to Joe and Betty. I had come down here full of hopes and plans for the future but these had come to nothing and I did not want to burden them with my problems for any longer. When I said this to Betty she assured me that I would be always welcome to stay as long as I needed to, but I thought to myself whether Joe would feel the same was as Betty did. She promised to talk to him and explain my position as I felt too embarrassed to do so, and maybe he could advise me the best way out of the quandary that I was in at present.

I did not sleep at all that night only tossed and turned endlessly trying to decide what I should do for the best and explain to Joe about my doubts for the future if I did return home. There was almost seven months to go before the baby was due so if I did not go back what could I do and where could I go till then? When morning finally came I was no closer to a decision. I would have to talk again with Joe then things might be clearer in my mind. The next evening after the children had gone to bed Joe, Betty and I went into the kitchen to talk things over. I explained how I felt and how worried I was and how I was going to cope until the baby was born. If I decided to bring up the baby on my own and did not go back to Glasgow, Joe said that there was no question of them turning me out, especially in my condition, and that I was welcome to stay with them until after the birth. But on the matter of me thinking of rearing the child myself he thought that I was mad even to consider that idea and that I had no conception of what I would be taking on. I said that I was still able to work and had enough money saved to keep me going in the meantime, but he replied that it was not a question of money but only doing the best for the baby and its future. In any case, he said, I had to tell John what the situation was and to give him the chance to say how he felt and what was going to happen in the future. I promised that I would get in touch with him and tell Joe about the outcome, and the matter was left there until this happened. True to my promise, I phoned John the following evening but as soon as he heard my voice he said, 'Well at last you have come to your senses' and, in the next breath, 'When are you coming back?'. In utter confusion I blurted out, 'I don't know', and before I could say anything more he said, 'Well if you don't know, nobody else does. But if you are not coming back and I am not coming to Corby again then I guess I have got my answer'. And with that he slammed the phone down before I could explain any further. How could I tell him now? I went into the room and told Joe what had happened. He offered to ring John himself and explain but I refused; this was my problem and I was the only one who could solve it.

Another sleepless night followed, but by morning I had come to a decision. I was not going back, as if I did John would know it was only because of the baby and not for his sake and the situation would be worse than it had been before. The only thing I was certain of was the fact that I wanted this baby and if this entailed me bringing it up on my own then so be it. I was young and healthy and able to work for my living, and if other women could do it so could I.

When I told Joe about what I had decided, he was very much against my decision. He told me that I did not know what a hard task I was taking on and that when I thought about it sensibly I would change my mind. He also said that nobody was going to give me any medals for what I was going to do and I would regret it in time. I knew he was only thinking of my welfare but I was determined to go ahead with what I had decided and nothing he said was going to alter my mind. In fact after all the turmoil of the last few weeks I suddenly felt calm and at peace with myself. I was not foolish enough to imagine that the road ahead would be smooth or easy going, and I knew there would be doubts about what the future would be for the baby and myself. But if things went wrong sometimes I would have nobody to blame but myself and I was willing to settle for that.

Chapter 14

To my surprise, the next few months passed very quickly and almost before I realised we were almost into the month of March, and that was the month that they had given me for the birth. I had booked into the new maternity unit that had recently been built in the town. I went there every week for a check up and everything was going very well for me and the baby. The morning sickness had stopped and actually I had never felt so well and healthy as I did then. I had not put on a lot of weight and they had told me that my baby would probably be quite small, but as long as it was healthy that was all that mattered to me. March the 17th, when I had been told I had been due, came and went and still nothing happened. So after another two weeks had passed, they decided that they would take me to the hospital to induce my labour. However a few days later, on the 6th April 1962, my labour pains started - not severe at first and just a few contractions - but at least the baby was now on its way.

Betty took me into the maternity unit as soon as Joe went to work at 6am, and stayed with me. The nurse that had been allocated to me told me that she needed another natural birth to make up her quota and, lucky me, I was the chosen one. The pains were now coming regularly but still not too severe and I remember thinking that all the stories I had been told about the agony of childbirth were very much exaggerated. This was nothing worse than a bad toothache. However, when the contractions started to become stronger, the nurse told Betty to go home and phone back in an hour or so when it would probably all be over. She had been with me for 6 hours and like me she had had no sleep the previous night and was exhausted. So she went back to the house to get lunch for the children, with me still in no great pain and still quite comfortable, and with the promise that she would phone as soon as she could manage. No sooner had she gone than the contractions became very severe and I did not feel serene or comfortable any longer. For almost two hours, that red-haired witch of a nurse kept me trying to bring the baby naturally when I had no strength left to do so. But at last she had to admit defeat and was forced to call an ambulance to take me into St. Mary's hospital in Kettering, where there was a resident surgeon which the new maternity unit lacked. In the ambulance the pain was really bad and the nurse told me to press hard on her hand when the need arose, and believe me I did just that. I don't think she could have had very much feeling left in that hand for quite a time after. I don't know if she ever got her quota, but at least she never got it from me.

When I reached the hospital they took me to the theatre and used forceps to deliver the baby. He weighed almost seven pounds, which was slightly below normal, but he was healthy and had all the normal necessities, so that was all that mattered. Betty told me later that she got the shock of her life when she phoned the unit expecting that the baby had been born, only to find that I was now in a hospital in Kettering. She had to wait for almost an hour before she received the news that I had a healthy baby boy and we were both doing well. I had six stitches after the birth and had to have a hot salt bath every day until the stitches were dissolved. In the meantime I had to carry a cushion with me everywhere I went so that I could sit down without discomfort.

The next day I was taken back to the unit in Corby, but before this happened I had a very frightening experience. Betty had come to Kettering to visit me as soon as she had heard of the birth. She had brought me some fruit and had peeled an orange for me and left it on my bedside table, I was so tired out that I had fallen asleep before she left and when I finally awoke I thought I was having a nightmare. My arm, which was hanging loosely outside the bed, was covered with dozens of little tiny creatures. I pinched myself had thinking it must be a dream that I was having, but it was all too real and they were still there. I screamed in terror and the nurse came running in. She said that the creatures were white ants and would not have harmed me. When Betty had left the orange on the table beside the bed the smell must have attracted them. This was an old hospital and I found out later that it was plagued with ants and other types of vermin. A new hospital was being built, but in the meantime the old one was being used if there was a shortage of beds elsewhere, and I was just unlucky that they had decided to pay a visit when I was on the premises. As I have said, I was taken back to Corby the next day, and what a difference! Everything in the unit was shining and new and I was put into a bed with an electric blanket and snowy white sheets.

I know every mother thinks her baby thinks is the most wonderful and best looking of all, and I was no exception. But he was really very cute. His hair was so fair it was almost white and his eyebrows were the same, and he had these greeny blue eyes and a cute button nose. His hair was short all over as if he had just had what was known then as a buzz cut, but to me he was the most handsome baby in the world. I know that it is said that babies cannot focus properly until they are a few weeks old but that night I woke up and looked inside the cot which was beside my bed and my baby was looking straight at me with a quizzical look in his eyes which seemed to say, 'Who are you and what am I doing here?'. It was the queerest sensation and it was at that moment that I bonded with my baby and that bond would never be broken.

In the ward beneath mine, another baby had been born, but this was not a joyful event such as mine had been. Little David, as he had been named was born without arms. Just stumps with finger-like things on the end. The first thalidomide baby born in Corby. His parents were only 17 years of age and had been only married for a year when he was born. His mother had originally come to Corby from London but after suffering from a very severe bout of morning sickness she had gone to London to stay with her mother for a few weeks and it was she who had taken her to the doctor to get something to relieve the symptoms. It was then that she had been prescribed a comparatively new drug which was called thalidomide, and this was the result. There were quite a few babies born afterwards who were born with the same symptoms, some with no arms and some with no legs or a light deformity. But as I said, this was the first case in Corby. The mother, whose name was May, was horrified when she saw the baby and could not accept what had happened. And who could blame her, as they were both so young and really just children themselves. The other patients had not been told about what had happened in case it upset them and were in total ignorance of the tragedy that had happened in our minds. But one night a few days after David's birth, May and her baby had come up to the ward to see another person who was there. It was close to the babies' bedtime and it was the custom then that you had to wrap your baby tightly in their shawl before you put them to sleep in their cot. This was an impossible task for me because as quickly as I wrapped my son up, the arms would go up, the shawl would be thrown off and instead of looking like a neat little bundle he would resemble an unmade bed. When May came that night David was neatly bundled up that I had to remark on it and said, 'How do you manage to keep David so neat and tidy?', and immediately May burst into tears and ran from the ward. Of course I had been ignorant of what had happened or I would never have said what I did. When the nurse told me why May had acted the way she did, I could have bitten my tongue off. How was I supposed to know what had happened to the baby when we were all in ignorance of thalidomide?

There is a happy ending to this sad tale. Because of David being the first case of thalidomide in Corby, the local paper kept an update of his progress. He had lots of painful operations as he grew older but eventually he was fitted with artificial arms which were as adaptable as real ones and he could use for every purpose. He was a clever child and did very well at school and eventually went to university. It was even mentioned in the paper saying what I did, but of course they did not name me. They did say that May did not bear me any ill will, as she knew that I was ignorant of the true facts of the case. In any case, she and her husband had long ago adapted to the tragedy of the baby's birth and were moving on and looking forward to a happy future for themselves and David. Of course, the story eventually moved out of the headlines, but at least we all knew now that things had turned out so much better that we could have envisaged all those years ago.

When the time came for the baby to be christened, we spent hours trying to decide what his name would be. Joe's children, Rose, Charlotte and young Joe, came up with some ridiculous ones as we went through the alphabet together, but eventually one of the girls suggested Raymond and I liked it immediately. I had not wanted a family name as there was so many Josephs and Roses already. But I did want Peter as a middle name, so we decided on Raymond Peter Wilkinson, and he was duly Christened as that. Betty had bought him a little lace outfit to wear to the Church and I had bought his shawl, so he looked a picture on that day. I still have his Christening robe to this day, almost fifty years after his birth.

When Raymond was a few months old I started working again. I had felt so guilty about Betty and Joe providing for me for so long but they had refused my offer of money when it was offered, At least now I could buy a few provisions to help out and it would make me feel at least I was contributing something to the family budget. Betty was not working at that time and said she would look after Raymond in the meantime so I could go out to work and we would see how things would work out. At least feeding the baby would not be a problem. He had been bottle fed from the very beginning and was thriving, as I knew that I would have to go to work and that breast feeding was not an option.

A few days previously I had noticed an advert in the local paper for a shop assistant wanted by the Home and Colonial Stores in the Market Square. So now that my child minding had been sorted out I decided to apply for the situation vacant. The shop was in a prime position right in the middle of the Market Square, a very busy and a popular store which had branches all over the Midlands. They sold all the usual groceries but they were famous for their fresh cold meat, bacon and chesses which were displayed in the window and were freshly cut daily. The shop was run by Mr Reeve and his wife. He did all the meat cutting and she made up the orders, of which there were many. I was interviewed by them both and gave them an account of my experience and I was given the job on the spot and told to start on the following Monday morning. My hours were from 9am till 6pm daily, with a Wednesday half day, 9am till 1pm, and the wages were £7.50 per week, quite a decent wage at that time. I was on a month's trial to see if I was suitable, and if so this would be a permanent situation. I went home very pleased that everything had gone so well and very glad to be one of the working class again.

I duly presented myself on Monday morning and was given an overall and introduced to the other full time worker whose name was Rena. She was about the same age as myself and seemed very nice. There was also a part time worker who only worked at weekends or any time that she was needed for extra shifts. My first day was spent learning prices and finding out about the merchandise and where it was situated and of course serving the customers. There were quite a few differences in the names of items that I had been accustomed to in Glasgow. For instance, there were five or six different types of bacon - short back, long back, green back and middle cut - whereas back home there were only two popular types, Ayrshire bacon and Belfast ham. So it took me some time to distinguish one from the other, but when I had to ask for advice Mr. Reeve was very helpful and said that I would soon learn to distinguish between the different cuts when I became familiar with them over time. Apart from this, I thought I had coped not too badly for my first day in and new job, or at least so I thought. But at the end of the day, Mr Reeve asked me to go into the back shop as he wanted to speak to me privately, and my confidence sunk without trace as I wondered what I had done to displease him. With a sinking heart I walked into the back room with him in fear and trembling and wondering if my working life there would be over before it started, but it turned out it was not as bad as I had feared.

During the morning I knew that he was watching every move I made, but that was quite usual with a new employee, and I could not think of anything that I had done to cause him displeasure. He told me to sit down and said, 'You must understand that we are here to serve the customers, and it is not their job to serve us'. I did not understand what he had meant and said so and I also added that I was sorry not to have given satisfaction in that if he wanted me to leave I would do so. He then said that this was furthest from his mind and he was quite satisfied with my work, but he had noticed something that had displeased him. One of my customers had asked for a bottle of lemonade which was on the shelf behind her, and as I was at the opposite side of the store I had asked her to pass it onto me so that I could put it with her order. This was the incident he was talking about. I apologised and he said that no more would be said about it, but he just wanted to make the point that we depended on our customers and that they did not depend on us, and he knew that I would remember this in the future which I assured him that I would. With this he bade me good night and said he would see me in the morning. So I left for home feeling slightly humbled and with my self confidence a little dented, but at least I still had a job.

The next few days passed smoothly and I felt that I was settling in very well and enjoying my work. On the Friday I met the other member of the staff. Her name was Corinne, a very attractive young lady with lovely dark eyes and black hair. She was in her 20's, and married with a small son. She was very chirpy and full of life, like the proverbial cockney sparrow which of course she was. She was a Londoner, she was a good worker and very popular with the customers, but her only fault was her unpunctuality; she was always late and running in at the last minute full of apologies. A few weeks later on a Saturday morning which was a very busy time for us she was more than half an hour late in appearing and Mr Reeve was very annoyed. At last she dashed in flustered and breathless and gasped, 'Oh Mr Reeve I am so sorry I have been so late, but it was not my fault'. Brian her husband had gone to work and some of their tropical fish had started having their babies. She had had to collect them as they were born, get a net and put them in another tank, or the other fish would have eaten them and he husband would never have forgiven her if that had happened. It turned out that Brian used to breed tropical fish as a hobby and was very devoted to his fish family. Mr Reeve just stood there with a look of amazement on his face whilst she was talking. He looked dumbstruck but when found his voice, he said, 'Well Corinne, over the months you have been here you have given me many and varied reasons for being late but having to ask for a midwife to a shoal of fish must be the oddest of them all'. He was trying to look angry but you could see he had difficulty in not laughing out loud and could only say, 'For God's sake, get your overall on and get some work done, your undoubted medical skills are no longer required'. And with that he hurried into the back shop, and Corrine got off with it again and left the rest of the staff helpless with laughter.

The next few months passed peacefully and uneventfully. I liked my job, Raymond was thriving, and the only minor drawback was that I had been saddled with a morning person, saddled being the operative word. It was not a problem getting Raymond down for his bed at night time, but it was a different matter getting him to stay there. Between 5 and 6 in the morning he would be wide awake and ready to play. He loved me to read stories to him and one of them was about a horse called Neddy. This story became his favourite and so this was his usual game in the morning; 'giddy up' he would say to me, as he jumped up and down on my stomach. Giddy I definitely was, but the up part was another problem. When the alarm clock went off a few hours later and I managed to unglue my eyelids I would think of the long and busy day ahead and groan, but I guess these are the joys of motherhood. When Raymond got his first tooth, took his first steps and sat up on his own for the first time I was not there to witness these things, and that was the down side of the coin for a working mother, a fact of life you must learn to accept. Oddly enough, when he began to crawl he did it backwards. I suppose like me he preferred doing things the hard way. It was not all work and no play for me as Rena my workmate and her husband were members of the Conservative Club who held dances every Saturday night and she and her husband invited me to join them there, Betty encouraged me to go and I really enjoyed the outings. There was a nice crowd there and they made me feel very welcome and it was something to look forward to at the end of the working week.

I stayed in my job for a year or so and was quite happy, but one of the customers was telling me about a job vacancy in the factory where she worked. It was better paid and a five day week and no Saturday work, so I decided to apply. The factory made cardboard boxes and was situated in Desborough, which was a few miles away but a bus was laid on for the workers from Corby who were picked up in the morning and brought back in the evening, and as the wages were much better than I was earning in the shop I thought this would be a good move for me. I was sorry to leave the shop as I had been very happy there, but I needed the extra money. Mr and Mrs Reeve gave me a very good reference and told me that if the new job did not come up to expectations I would be welcome back anytime, which was very kind of them and much appreciated.

I started in the factory the following week, the card board came in flat packs and we had to fold them into the shape of boxes and then fasten them together in a machine which had steel pins to secure them. I had never worked in a factory before and found it very boring. I missed the customers and the daily chit-chat with them, but there was one upside to the job, the staff were all female except for the foreman, Cyril, and every hour a bell would tinkle and we would all troop off to the toilet for a ten minute break. They must have thought that we were all incontinent or something needing a toilet break so often, although most of us used this time to have a quick smoke. On a Friday afternoon there was hardly any work done at all and from about 3 o'clock till finishing time the women would all gather in the toilets where they would do one another's hair or pluck eyebrows or get beautified in some way for the coming weekend. It was so different from what I had been used to in the working world, but who was I to complain.

One night when I arrived home Betty was really upset and told me that Raymond had been sick all afternoon. He had seen some cigarette butts in the ash tray and picked them up and put them in his mouth and that was the result. Joe and I both smoked in the house as most people did at that time, so either of us could have been the culprit and poor Raymond was the sufferer, so we knew we would have to be] more careful in the future. I told one of my workmates about this the next day and she said, 'Well at least he will never suffer from worms.' I don't know if this was supposed to reassure me of the aftermath of his actions but at least Raymond was alright the next day and that was a relief at least.

Looking back I find it is not the big things in life that stick in your mind and that bring you to the cross roads where you have to make a big decision that will change everything, not the tragedies or calamities but the little pin pricks that make us stop and consider where we are going, and if we are heading in the right direction to arrive at our chosen destination. In my case it happened one wet Sunday evening when I was on my way to church. The rain had lasted all day and the road was wet and slippery as I made my way up Beanfield Avenue to evening mass. Suddenly my foot got caught in a pothole in the road, I tripped and almost fell and the heel came off my shoe. As I squelched along miserably I suddenly thought, 'What am I doing here and where am I going in my life?'. I have no home of my own, hardly any money to spend and what future am I making for my child. Suddenly a grey cloud seemed to come over me and all I wanted to do was sit on the wet road and cry my eyes out, and Joe's words came back to me, 'Nobody is going to give you a medal for what you are doing'. I did not want a medal, only a ray of hope that I was doing the right thing for me and my child and at that moment life seemed as dark as the clouds above my head.

Of course the black mood passed as moods always do, but the main problem still remained as to where do I go from here. I had been staying with Joe and Betty for over a year, the children were growing up and the girls especially needed their space which I was occupying. The answer came suddenly and most unexpectedly. Our church ran a weekly sweepstake which Joe, Betty and I ran every week and I struck lucky a few weeks afterwards when I found that I had the lucky ticket and won first prize which was £50.00 - maybe not a lot of money these days but to me it seemed like a lot of money at the time. I was wondering what the best way was of spending the money when Betty came up with a surprising solution when she said, 'Why don't you have a break and go to Glasgow and see your friend Ina. It will do you good to get away for a time and give you a breathing space for you decided what you want to do in the future'.

I had already spoken to Betty about having to find a permanent home for Raymond and I as the present situation could not go on indefinitely and nothing seemed to be turning up in Corby, where they were giving preference to families whose husbands were in the steel works.

Betty had said there was no rush to change things but I knew in her heart that she agreed with me in this matter. She also knew that I was not happy in my present job and this was making things worse. She told me she would continue looking after Raymond until I had found a job and a place to live and would bring him to me when I was ready and settled. I could not believe how kind and considerate she was and immediately took her up on her offer. I wrote to Ina immediately and received her answer a few days later. She told me that I would be welcome to stay at her house as long as I needed to. Her eldest son Norman and his wife were emigrating to New Zealand shortly so there was plenty of room for me. I put my notice in at the factory and left there a week later. So now all I had to do was pack my stuff and leave. It was heartbreaking for me saying goodbye to the family as they had been so good to me, but I knew it would not be forever and I was leaving Raymond in good hands and with people he knew and loved. He was too young to understand that I was going away and I tried to comfort myself by saying it was for his own sake as well as mine that I was doing this. But it did not make it any easier as my heart was breaking as I kissed him goodbye.

When I arrived in Glasgow, Ina was waiting for me and took me to her house in Croftfoot, a sprawling estate on the outskirts of Glasgow. It was a Corporation house and consisted of three bedrooms, a bathroom and kitchen and, as there was only Ina, her husband and her youngest son living at the house, there was ample room for me. I did not feel in the way or that I was pushing anyone out and in any case I was only intending to stay for a week or two until I found something more permanent. My first priority was to go round the factor's offices and put my name down on their housing lists and hope that something would turn up quite soon. I started this on the following week and I stressed that anything would do; one or two bedrooms, or even a bedsit as long as it was a permanent tenancy and the place where we could be settled for the future. I knew I would need all the money I still had in the post office, so I sent in my bank book and asked them to clear the account and leave just enough to keep the book open, and to send me the remainder. I was delighted a few days later to receive my money plus the interest which had accrued over the period and which I had not withdrawn and this came to almost £40.00. It was a godsend to me as with the sweepstake money and my savings, there was enough to last me for a few months until I found a job, and hopefully a house also.

Ina was still going to the old-time dancing and took me with her the following week to meet her other friends. There was Neil, who was her usual dancing partner, and another married couple, and amazingly, someone I already knew, Jackie Crawford. I had known him and his sister Betty from my time when I stayed in Bonawe Street, where I had my first house after I was married. Betty had been a cleaner in the shop at the corner of the street and we became quite friendly. She stayed just a few streets away and had introduced me to her brother, Jackie, and her father who also stayed locally. It was so nice to see another familiar face and we had a good gossip about what had happened since we last met. Jackie was very easy to talk to and I told him about staying in Corby and now coming back to Glasgow trying to find a place to rent. He told me he was staying with his father who was now a widower, and when I told him about leaving my name in the different factors' offices waiting list, he said that if I wished he would put in a good word for me at his factor's office also, as his father had been a tenant there for almost forty years. I thanked him and said I would be very grateful if he would do so as every little helped, and as the more places that knew of me, the better chance I would have of something turning up in the future.

I really enjoyed my night out and it was so nice meeting Jackie again after such a long time. As I mentioned before, Ina's sister was a manageress in

Ross's Dairy in town, and when Ina told her about me looking for a job she promised that she would let me know if any vacancies turned up in shop work, as she knew that I had plenty of experience in that trade. So that was another door that might be opened for me.

I wrote and told Betty about what had been happening and enquiring about Raymond. She said that he was fine and he was missing me. When I got my money from the post office I sent him a toy dog with a leash on which you could pull it along and when she told him it was a present from me he immediately named it Horsy, and trailed it along everywhere he went.

A few weeks later Ina told me that, true to her word, her sister had mentioned my name to some of her bosses and asked them to let them know if any vacancies occurred, and it turned out there was now a vacancy in one of the town shops for a manageress. She told me I should apply for the job and with her recommendation I would have a good chance of getting the job. Shortly afterwards that's what happened. The manageress had been retiring and they had been looking for a replacement. I got an interview a few days later and was offered the job. The wages were good and would give the chance to save for the time when I managed to get a house.

But suddenly my feelings of relief of getting the job evaporated. The main problem of where I was going to stay was still unsolved. I had the job but I could not work until I got a place to stay for Raymond and myself, so I was no further on than I was before. When I said this to Ina, she suggested putting Raymond in day nursery that I could leave him in the morning before going to work and pick him at night when I finished. In the meantime I could stay with her as Raymond and I would only be there at night time and would not affect her living arrangements at all. There was a nursery quite near where she lived and she said that it had a good

153

reputation, so I should try it and if everything went well then my problem would be solved.

I wrote to Betty and told her about getting the job and about Ina's suggestion about the nursery and asked her to bring Raymond to Glasgow as soon I had got a place for him at the nursery. She wrote back and advised me that it would be better to wait until he was happy there before I made any permanent decision about his future, but that she would bring him to Glasgow the following week, as at least I had a place for us to stay in the meantime.

I managed to get a place for him in the nursery and Betty arrived the following week with Raymond, I could not believe how much he had grown in a couple of months that we had been separated from each other. He was a little shy with me at first but I suppose that was natural. He called me 'mummy' and he called Betty 'mummy Betty', and that upset me a little, but he must have been a bit confused with all that had been happening to him. Betty was staying with my brother John and Marie for a few days. She wanted to see how Raymond settled in the nursery before she went back home.

The first morning I took him he was very quiet and subdued when I left him, but when I got to the door he clung to me and cried. The lady in charge said not to worry and he would be alright once I had gone, but when I went to collect him that evening when he saw me he burst into tears and rushed towards me, clinging to me and sobbing. The second morning it was more or less the same thing as when we arrived at the door he said, 'I don't want to go in there'.

I did not know how to cope with this situation, but when I thought about it afterwards I realised how cruel and unfeeling I had been. I had taken him away from everyone and everything that was familiar to him and brought him to a strange place and people who were strangers also and then left him for hours in another alien situation, and in his childlike mind there would be the fear that I would not return to claim him. I had left him before and I might do it again and he would be on his own.

Betty was as upset as I was and she felt she could not go home and leave things the way they were. I could not concentrate on my job with the worry of Raymond being so unhappy, and everything seemed in such a mess. I had thought I had everything planned out but again I had got it all wrong. As our national Bard Rabbie Burns once said, 'The best laid schemes of mice and men gang aft agley, and leave us nought but grief and pain for promised joy'. These words were so true in my case. That evening Betty got in touch with the rest of the family and asked them to come to John's house to decide what to do about the situation. She told them that I needed a permanent home where Raymond would feel secure and that he needed me to be there with him until I managed to get a house for both of us. They would have to decide where that home would be. My brother Peter would be the ideal person to provide this as he had a room and he was on his own in the house, but I knew he was not used to having a child running around and was used to having his privacy and the freedom to do his own thing. So I did not think he would take it kindly to having us thrust upon him. It was very embarrassing for me to be there while they were discussing my future, so I said that I would take Raymond to Ina's house for the night, and I said they could let me know what they had decided on the following day when I returned. The following day I was told that Peter had agreed that Raymond and I could stay with him until I got a place of my own. At last Betty was able to go home with an easier mind.

The next few weeks were tranquil and stress-free. Peter was at work all day, so Raymond and I had the house to ourselves. There was a garden for him to play in and Jean and Sam's youngest daughter would come in after school each day to play with him while I did the housework and prepared the evening meal. We - Peter, Raymond and I - all sat down to eat together and if Peter was staying in I would take Raymond up to bed after our meal so as to give Peter some privacy to watch the television or do whatever he wanted to do in the evening in peace and quiet, while I read stories to Raymond while he fell asleep. This was a very restful time for me. It was like finding an oasis in the desert, a springing up of hope after the drought of the last few weeks. Of course I had to give up my job and I felt very badly about letting Ina's sister down when she had been so helpful in getting me the position, but Ina had explained the situation to her and she was very understanding, so that was something less for me to worry about.

Raymond was back to his usual self, and things were turning out far better than I had hoped or expected. We spent our first Christmas there in 1963 and Raymond received twenty two presents. Peter counted them all and there were tears in his eyes as he said, 'I never thought he would receive so many presents from so many people'. Like my father he was very emotional where children were concerned. Of course there were presents that had come from Corby and from all my family in Glasgow, so he had not been forgotten by anyone. Peter and I had to laugh as he was looking at all the presents and did not know which one to play with and ended up eventually crawling in and out of a big box that had contained some motors and enjoying himself hugely. I suppose that is typical of children. They don't really need very expensive presents to keep them happy; it's usually the little things that give them the most pleasure. Looking back on my life I have been very fortunate. I have had many good friends and a close family and when things seemed at their worst there was always someone there for me to pick me up when I stumbled and put me back on my feet again, and I thank God for them all.

The next few weeks passed very smoothly and Raymond and I settled in to a quiet and peaceful routine and for the first time in months I was sleeping soundly at night time, untroubled by what the morning would bring. I had been staying with Peter for a couple of months when I received a letter from Ina informing me that there was a house being vacated the following month in the block of flats beside Jackie's father. It consisted of a room and kitchen which was ample for us, and if I was interested I had to get in touch with Jackie to set a date when I could meet him and he would take me to meet the factor to introduce me and to fill in the appropriate forms to secure the vacancy. I was so delighted that I could barely contain my excitement till Peter got home so that I could tell him the good news. Oddly enough he did not seem very pleased and only said, 'Well, there is not any great hurry to move out, is there?'. I was amazed at his reaction but when I thought about it afterwards I realised that it must have been quite a lonely life or him, coming home to an empty house after his day's work and cooking his evening meal and nobody to talk to about the day's happenings. Although Raymond I may not have been great company for him at least there was always a hot meal ready and the house was warm and lived in during the day, when otherwise it would have been cold and empty, so I could get a little of what he was feeling about my news. Maybe the benefits were not all on my side. I would always be grateful to him for providing us for a home when we needed one so badly, but I longed for a place of my own and this was the chance that I had hoped for, so I had to grab it with both hands. I wrote to Ina right away and arranged for a day to meet Jackie the following week. I did not tell Betty at the time as I wanted to wait until I definitely got the house before raising her hopes and then if things did not go too well having to dash them down again.

I met Jackie as arranged and he took me to the factor's office to meet him. The factor was an elderly man and was very friendly in his manner. He told me what the rent would be, which was very reasonable, and then took me to see the flat. These flats had three storeys, and I was on the second floor. The interior was very clean and did not need much decoration, but as was usual at that time in Glasgow, there was no inside toilet. But as I had expected this to be the case, I was not unduly disappointed. At least the toilet was spotlessly clean and there was even a curtain on the small window. It was the tenant's job to clean the stairs and the toilet at least once a week on a rota basis, and it looked as if my neighbours were doing a good job. Jackie told me that his other sister Hannah occupied the flat immediately above me and as I had met her before, I would not be totally amongst strangers. Of course Jackie and his father were in the next block, so that was an added bonus. The factor then checked on a few details of my previous addresses. There were a few forms to sign, I paid a month's rent in advance, and was given the keys and told that I could move in the following month. I could not believe how lucky I had been to have received the tenancy so easily, but it was only because Jackie and his father had been good tenants for so long and they had vouched for me, and that had made all the difference. I was walking on air as I left that office, knowing that I was now a tenant of a flat in 24 Cameron Street, Maryhill, Glasgow. It was a marvellous feeling, a place of my own at last. At that moment I would not have changed places with the Queen in her palace.

Chapter 15

A month later we moved in. I used the last of my savings to buy linoleum for the kitchen floor and a small rug for the front of the fire, plus the usual kitchen utensils, kettle, teapot and cutlery etc.. The biggest item was the cooker which was well passed its usable date, and this was a necessity. But again my family turned up trumps. They all put together to buy me a new one, and also helped with bedding, curtains, towels etc.. As usual the two beds were set into the wall, a set-in bed, so that saved quite a bit of expense, I also managed to buy some second-hand kitchen chairs and two small arm chairs, so I now had the necessities for daily living. What would we do without our family, that beloved octopus whose tentacles hold us close together and, although the bonds slack with the passing of time, never really set us free?

Money was now my biggest problem. The rent had to be paid and food had to be bought, and I could not depend on my family's charity forever. They had already done more than enough for me. I would not be able to work for at least a couple of years till Raymond started school, so how was I to manage till that time? I was discussing this with Betty, Jackie's sister, and she advised me to go the social security office to see if I was eligible for some help. I knew nothing about benefits and social security. I had never been on the dole as I was always able to work, so this was new territory for me.

A few days later, trembling with nerves and with my stomach doing somersaults, I went to the benefits office. At the back of my mind were the tales my mother used to tell me of my Aunt Agnes whose husband was unable to work and they had to go on the poor relief, or The Parish as it was then called, and how they had to sell everything except the absolute necessities before they were allowed a few shillings every week. But as it happened it was not as bad as I had feared. I had to give my name to a clerk at the counter and she told me I would be called when someone was free to interview me. I took a seat on the hard bench against the wall where a dozen or more people were already waiting, and after about fifteen minutes my name was called and I went to a small cubicle where a lady was waiting to interview me. She asked a lot of questions about my circumstances, what savings I had if any, what my rent was and how long I had been at my present address. She was quite pleasant and after she had taken notes of my answers she informed me that she would be in touch in a few days time to let me know the outcome. I was so glad to get out of that stuffy room and into the fresh air again and I said a little prayer to myself as I walked home that things would turn out well and I would get a bit of help to keep us going until I was able to earn a wage again. I received a letter after a few days to say that I had been awarded £3. 4 shillings, which was £3.20 a week. This was just enough to pay my rent and, if I was very careful, to cover the price of our food. It was not a lot but to me it was a godsend and I was very grateful for it.

I had never intended for Raymond to be ruled by a petticoat government. I wanted to always to have a male presence in his life, someone to kick a ball about with and all the other manly things that boys expect their father to do with them. In the beginning there was Joe to fill this role and now suddenly there was Jackie taking over. He and Raymond liked the same things and bonded immediately. In the summer evenings Jackie would take him to the park or for a long walk. They both loved books and also Jackie introduced him to jigsaw puzzles which soon became a passion with him. He also

160

took him to the local swimming baths and taught him to swim, starting him off doing the doggie paddle until he became confident in the water, and in a short time was swimming on his own.

As I mentioned before, Jackie's sister Hannah stayed in the flat above me. She had a small daughter Marie who was only a year or so older than Raymond and she spent a lot of time in my house playing with him. Hannah worked part time in a bakery and sometimes Marie would stay with me for a few hours while her mother was at work and after a few months Hannah asked me if I would take care of her on a daily basis and she would pay me for doing so. She offered me £1.50 per week and this would be a big help to me financially, but I was afraid to accept in case it might affect my benefit money and said that I would have to check out the benefit office before I agreed to do so. I trudged the couple of miles to the office and waited again to be interviewed. I explained to the interviewer why I was there and that I was worried about my benefits being affected if I took on extra paid work. She smiled and said that I was allowed to earn another £2.00 without my money being affected. So I could have saved myself a long walk if I had known about this, but I had never been told. But at least now I knew the score for the future and that was the main thing.

On the first day of my childcare duties things did not go as smoothly as I had hoped. My usual daily programme was a trip to the newsagents where I would buy my morning paper, my usual ten cigarettes and Raymond would get his usual treat of a small bar of chocolate. Of course Marie had to get her chocolate too. On the way back home we passed an ice cream shop and Marie demanded an ice cream, which I told her she could not have as she already had had her chocolate treat. She immediately threw a tantrum, laying on the pavement and screaming at the top of her voice. I knew that Hannah had been in the habit of giving her money to keep her quiet when she was leaving for work, but I was not in a position to do this and had no intention of starting it, Raymond and I walked on and left her screaming on the ground but I kept a wary eye on her to make sure she did not come to any harm, I knew if I gave in to her that I was setting a pattern for the future, and this I did not intend to do. After about ten minutes or so with the passersby staring at me and tut tutting, the tantrum ended and Marie had run out of steam. The tearful child ran after me sobbing, 'I am sorry Auntie Netta, I am sorry'. I took her hand and said, 'I forgive you Marie, but don't ever do that to me again or I won't be taking care of you anymore'. Thankfully she never did and things went smoothly afterwards. I looked after her for more than a year until she started school, by which time she was so much a part of my family that her mother had to drag her upstairs at night time screaming that she wanted to stay with Raymond and I.

Hannah was a very good-hearted person but she was terrible manager where money was concerned. I was paid my benefit money every Monday and she received her wages on a Friday plus her husband's wages, but almost every week she would run out of money and would ask me for a loan until her wages were paid. She always paid me back what she owed me, and on the rare occasion when she was off work and did not really need my help she never stopped my money. Every Friday she would bring me something nice for tea, like a cream sponge or a packet of biscuits. I was always also very lucky with my new neighbours. The lady living immediately across the landing from me was a lovely person and very kind to Raymond and I. Her name was Jessie McIver. She had never married and stayed with her brother Angus, or Angie as she called him, and her elderly mother. They were of Highland descent and were all lovely people. She was always handing in something

162

for Raymond and I; scones, cakes or biscuits for our tea and to spare my feelings, always excuses that she had baked too many or Angie did not like them and they would be wasted otherwise. But I knew this was to save me feeling I was receiving charity. One week Angie won £50 on the Rangers football pools and immediately handed me £2 for me to buy something for Raymond, or 'the little man' as he called him. I was so lucky to be living amongst such generous and kindly people. I was also friendly with the lady on the upper landing, her name was Margaret Goodhall, and she was about the same age as myself. Her marriage had broken up and ended in divorce a few years previously. She had two sons, Edward and Brian. Edward, the elder one, was about 10 years of age and Brian was just starting school at 5 years old. She had a steady boyfriend and they were hoping to get engaged in the near future. I had now been living in Cameron Street for almost 2 years and it had been a very happy period in my life in which I had made some very good friends.

In December 1966, Jackie's sister Betty was having a New Year Party to which all her neighbours and friends had been invited and these included me and Margaret Goodhall. The house was absolutely crammed with people and we had a marvellous night. One of the guests, a man called Alec Lamb who was a friend of the family, immediately attached himself to Margaret who was a very attractive woman and monopolised her for all the evening, flirting with her and paying her compliments. When the party was over she told me that he had invited her to go out with him to the dancing. She told me that she would love to go but not knowing him very well she was a bit wary of going out as a couple and asked me if I would come with her for support. I told her that I did not want to play gooseberry but she was very insistent and I was sorely tempted. It had been such a long time since I had gone out socially and I knew that Jackie's niece would gladly babysit for me, so finally I agreed, little knowing that by making this decision I was creating a turning point in my life.

There was a dance hall called Barrowland where they held a weekly dance for the over 25's, and this was where was Margaret and Alec had decided to go for their evening out, with me in tow. When we arrived at the hall Alec went to the bar for drinks and returned later accompanied by another man whom he introduced as John Clark. It transpired that they had both been long distance drivers on the buses and knew each other very well, but had not been in touch for a few years until this chance meeting. We all stood chatting for a few minutes while I weighed up this friend of Alec's. He was quite tall and well built with a very pleasant face and a nice speaking voice. Margaret and Alec got up to dance which left the two of us on our own. I wished that he would either ask me to dance or go away and give me the chance to find another partner. Eventually he did take the hint and we went onto the dance floor. He was quite a good dancer and very easy to talk to. So we all stayed together as a group for the rest of the evening, occasionally changing partners, Margaret with John and Alec with me, but of the two I preferred to dance with John as I found Alec to be a bit of a bore and full of his own importance. At the end of the evening Alec asked Margaret if she would come out with him again, but she suggested that we join forces and go out as a foursome, if John and I were agreeable. John said yes immediately when this was suggested, so the final decision was left to me and as I had enjoyed his company and there was safety in numbers I agreed. We went out together another couple of times, but Betty, Jackie's sister, told Margaret that Alec was a married man of which she had been ignorant, so she decided to end the friendship. She had been carried away by the flattery and the compliments but realised there was no future in it and it was not worth compromising her relationship with her steady boyfriend, and made the wise decision not to see Alec again. John asked me if I would still go out with him as a couple and by this time I had learned to trust him and feel safe in his company, so I said that I would like to do that.

He had told me a little of his circumstances. He had been a widower for two years since his wife had died suddenly, leaving a family of five children, three girls who were teenagers, a boy of almost 17, and one of 20 who had just married and whose wife was expecting their first child. One of the girls, the eldest, was working and living away from home but the rest of them were still staying in the family house. I felt so sorry for him; he was only a young man, 38 years of age, and had been left a very heavy burden to carry on his own. I had told him of my position and he was very understanding and kind. I had also made it clear there could be no happy ending for us as I would never be free to marry again, but he said that we could still be friends and let the future take care of itself and I told him I would be happy and agreeable to do that.

My sister Chris's husband David was due to go on another tour of Germany in April 1967 and she asked me if I would like to go there for a few weeks holiday. At that time, she and her husband were planning to have a romantic weekend in Paris while they were there and she wanted me to be there for the children while they were away. I, of course, was delighted to do so and Raymond I were very excited at the prospect of a holiday abroad, and immediately started packing for the trip. When I told John of my plans he was a little crestfallen as I would be away for a few weeks, but he agreed that it would be a lovely break for Raymond and me.

John had a little car and he said he would take me to the airport to save me the expense of hiring a taxi and I was delighted to accept his offer. Chris and David met us at the airport when we landed in Germany and it was lovely to see them and the children again. Before they set off on their trip to Paris they introduced me to Gerry, their friend and neighbour who was going to keep an eye on me while they were away and whom I had to contact if I was in doubt or worried about anything. As soon as they had gone off the boys decided they would have a game of cricket and Raymond went along with them too. A few minutes later there was a hammering on the door and when I opened there were the boys frightened and shaking with nerves and Raymond with blood pouring from an open wound above his eyebrow. He had been standing too close to the wicket and when Jeremy, my nephew, had swung his bat Raymond got the full force of it on his face.

I grabbed him and ran to Gerry's house and he put us both in his car and ran us to the military hospital a few miles away. When we got there the doctor said he would have to have a few stitches and asked me to hold his head steady while he inserted them. But when I saw the needle coming towards the gaping wound I started to shake with nerves and Gerry had to take over. Raymond did not cry at all while the treated him but I felt every stitch going into that wound. Even now, more than forty years later, that scar still shows deep and white if Raymond is tired and worried about anything. The rest of our holiday went smoothly and we had a wonderful time and of course Raymond was soon back to normal and in fact I think he was quite proud of his war wound. A friend of my sister had her brother staying with while he was on holiday from London. He was Secretary to the Archbishop of Westminster who had kindly given him the use of his car while he was on holiday. When he heard that we were both returning to London on the same day he offered us a lift from the airport to catch our train from Euston Station, so Raymond and I travelled in style through London in the Archbishops car, a fitting to an unforgettable holiday.

When we arrived back John was waiting at the airport and drove us home, and what a wonderful surprise awaited us. While we were away he had papered and painted my kitchen, going straight from work each evening and working there for a few hours. Jessie McIvar had my spare key and would let him and lock up when he was finished. She even supplied him with tea and cakes when he was on the job. He had bought two beautiful cut glass vases and filled them with fresh flowers for our arrival. What a lovely gesture, and what a kind and generous person he was. I still have those vases on my sideboard after all these years. John was not only kind to me; Raymond was included in many of our outings. At that time *The Sound Of Music* was the film that everyone wanted to see, and John managed to get tickets for the Saturday matinee so Raymond could come too. It was these little gestures that meant so much and endeared him to me.

While on holiday in Germany I had celebrated my 43rd Birthday. Chris and David had booked a table for a dinner dance to be held at the Officers' Mess and to which they could invite their family or friends. When we arrived the festivities were in full swing and there was a German band playing the music. This was of the 'oom-pa-pa' variety which immediately set your feet tapping to the rhythm. We sat chatting for a few minutes enjoying the atmosphere when suddenly from a nearby table a gentleman arose and came across to our table. He clicked his heels, bowed to David and said to him while looking at me, 'Would the young lady care to dance?'. David looked at me and I said yes. So the gentleman offered me his arm and led me onto the dance floor. He was German but spoke perfect English. He was a good dancer and we did a kind of Polka around the floor. We stayed there for another couple of dances, which I enjoyed. Then he took me back to my table, again, a short bow to David and a thank you to me, and then went back to his friends. I thought how quaint and old fashioned it was but rather nice to be treated so courteously and David explained that this was the usual custom over there. If the lady was not with a partner then the older man in the group was always asked for permission for the person to dance with the intended lady. It was quite a different approach from what I was used to in Glasgow where usually a look and then a nod in the direction of the dance floor was considered enough of a request for the pleasure of your company. Most of the young Glaswegian men would never have graduated from the charm school.

There was so many changes in Germany since the last time I had visited there a few years after the war. At that time there was lots of signs of the devastation that had occurred and the German people looked tired and rather shabby. But that had all changed now; everywhere you looked there were new buildings and smart fashionable stores selling luxury goods of all kinds and full of well-dressed and prosperous customers. The other thing that struck me was the cleanliness of the streets. There was never a trace of litter of any kind to be found. It was the same thing in Holland when I accompanied my sister over the border to do her weekend shopping. Unfortunately nobody could say the same thing of the large cities of Britain and I can now understand why we were called the dirty man of Europe. Understandably, there was never any love lost between the British people and the German people, but no one can deny that they were a very clean race. Every morning when I walked into town with Chris I would see these pillow like objects hanging out of windows to air. When I asked Chris what they were, she said they were called duvets, or, as we called them, continental quilts. I had heard of them but they had as yet not become popular in Britain. We were still using sheets, blankets and heavy quilts for our bedding and I could not see the fashion of lightweight duvets catching on in our country. How wrong I was, as they are now an essential item in every British home, but this was the first time that I had encountered them so I will always associate them with Germany and my holiday there.

The following September, in 1967, Raymond started school and I worried as all mothers do about how he would settle in to the new environment. I had done as much ground work as possible to make it easier for him. He could count and read the smaller words in his books and tell the time by the clock. This was more of a pleasure than a chore to me as he was so eager to learn and so quick on the uptake. The first morning when I took him to school I fully expected a few tears as I left him there, but my fears were groundless. He waved goodbye, took his teacher's hand, and walked off to the classroom without a backward glance, and I was the one with tears in my eyes as he left. When I picked him up at lunchtime, as the new intake only had morning lessons, he was chatting away about what he had been doing and looking forward to going back the next day. So I knew I could relax and stop worrying about him. I took him back and forward to school for a couple of weeks and then he announced that he wanted to go by himself in future. I was a bit doubtful of this at first, but as his school was only a few streets away and there was a lollipop lady at the only point where he had to cross the road, I reluctantly agreed but made him promise that he would always wait for the lady to take him across the road. As it happens he did not have to go on his own after all; one of the mothers I used to have a chat with when we were leaving the children off at school asked me if her little girl could call for Raymond each morning and walk to school with him until she was confident enough to go to school on her own, and I agreed immediately as it was one less thing to worry about. On the first morning that this happened I watched from the bedroom window as Raymond took the little girl's hand and walked along the road chatting to her and I felt so proud to be his mum. Raymond loved school and made quite a few new friends. One of them was a poor little scrap who always looked as though he was half-starved, and had a constant drip at his nose and never seem to have a hanky to wipe it with, which I had to supply on a daily basis. Raymond would bring him home after school where I would feed them both with tea and biscuits. This little boy had his lunch as school and was supplied with tickets to pay for it. I had been told that I was also allowed this due to my circumstances, but I did not avail myself of the offer. After all, how much did it cost to feed a child of 5 years of age and in any case I did not want him to be any different from any of his mates. The months passed very happily and before I knew it, Raymond was ready to start on his next adventure: the Big School as he called it, and was not an infant any longer. Now his education was moving up to another level.

I had been going out with John now for a couple of months and had met his family. Mary, the youngest at almost 16 years of age, was a typical child of the 60's, mini-skirted, rebellious and always trying to push the boundaries in order to get more freedom for herself. Charles, the only boy still at home and now 17, was in his first job and now at the crossroads between boyhood and manhood, a very difficult place to be, trying to act like an adult but now and then showing glimpses of a little boy lost and not too sure what category he belonged to. Cath, at 18, was working in an office and was more assured in her manner and took herself very seriously, and Ann, the oldest of the girls at 20, was now working as a conductress on the buses and was still living away from home. She had come to visit me a couple of times when she was on the Maryhill route. She was different from the other two girls, very cheery and talkative and we got along quite well. John, the oldest of the family as I mentioned before, was married and he and his wife were expecting their first baby. He was a miniature of his father in looks and temperament, although much smaller in stature. I had only met him a few times but he seemed very a sensible and a steady type. As one would imagine with three teenagers still living at home, housekeeping was not the top of their agenda and the house was not kept in tip-top order, so I suggested to John that I came to the house now and then and do a bit of cleaning for him, I knew he did his best but with a full-time job plus shopping, washing and cooking, he had quite enough on his plate. When I mentioned this, he suggested that I come up at the weekends as this would give me a break also and as we normally went out on a Saturday night it would save me paying for a baby sitter as there were enough people at the house to look after Raymond. So it was agreed that he would pick me up on a Friday night after work and take me back on a Monday morning in time for Raymond starting school. After a time this became the usual occurrence. I would do the washing, tidy around and make an occasional meal for the family. After a short time the house was looking a lot better and John really appreciated my efforts. I was in a difficult position with regards to the family. I was not trying to act like a substitute mother, as they were too old for that, and I had no ambition to fill that role in any case. But as long as we did not actually dislike each other and managed to rub along that was as much as I could wish for and I think we managed to do that at least. Of all the family Raymond seemed to prefer Charles, which I suppose was natural, and they got on very well together. At that time the Beatles were all the rage and Charles would spend time teaching Raymond the words and the actions of their songs, and stand there with a proud look on his face as Raymond performed. The girls were very good with him also, but at that time Charles was the favourite in his eyes.

As I said John and I used to go to a dinner dance at Reo Stakis restaurant on a Saturday evening and the first night this happened Charles was left in charge of Raymond. Raymond was not too happy to be left, but John assured me that he would be alright once we were gone, so I reluctantly agreed. When we returned to the house the first person I saw was Charles out on the street playing football with his pals and when I asked him where Raymond was he had said he had left him in the bath. I dashed up the stairs and into the bathroom with visions of Raymond who was unused to a big bath on his own slipping down between the water, but thankfully he was quite happy splashing about and spraying water everywhere. But I gave Charles a lecture about it and told him never to do that again and he apologised, although I think he thought to himself that I was making a big fuss about nothing and I suppose I was, but I suppose that's what mothers do where their children are concerned.

A few weeks later John amazed me by suggesting we should become engaged. I said that I thought that this would serve no purpose as there was no chance of me ever being free to marry, but he said that he wanted to show that we were a couple and serious about one another. When I told him about my reservations he said that I had never been in touch with a lawyer to see if there was any chance of me being granted a divorce on the grounds of separation, as it was now nearly seven years since we had last been in contact. I explained that even if I did manage to get a divorce on these grounds I still would not be able to get married in a Catholic church as a divorce was not recognised and I would not feel properly married if we went anywhere else. The only other way out was to be granted an annulment but to get this was almost an impossibility but John said that I should get in touch with a Catholic lawyer and find out what my chances were and to this I agreed without any conviction of its success.

I found the address and phone number of a lawyer in the Catholic directory, a Mr Ross Harper, and phoned to make an appointment. I was not looking forward to the interview and was dreading all the personal questions that were certain to be asked of me. When I met the lawyer I was not very impressed with him; he seemed very off hand in his manner and I did not feel comfortable talking to him. When I asked him questions about getting an annulment he replied that this was a very remote possibility. There were very few annulments granted and before they were I would have to go in front of a panel and prove to their satisfaction that the marriage was null and void and there was no hope of a reconsideration. And even if I had managed to convince him of this, the procedure would take a long time before anything was finalised as the findings had to be sent to Rome to the Pope's secretary before a decision could be made and this could take months or even years before it was over. Even then, if I did get an annulment there was still a divorce to get through before I was free to marry again.

I felt that I had made a useless journey and was getting nowhere but the lawyer asked me to make an appointment for the following week where we could go in to the matter more deeply as there was still a lot of questions to be answered by me before he decided if he had any chance of success and if it was worthwhile for him to accept the case. I left the office feeling absolutely deflated and wondering if it was all worthwhile coming to see him again as I did not feel that anything could be gained by continuing when all seemed so hopeless. But I had promised John that I would give it a trial and would not give in at the first hurdle. So I made the appointment as he had suggested but went away with a horrible feeling that I was fighting a losing battle and one that I had no chance of winning.

When I returned the following week the lawyer informed me that he had been making some enquiries about a possible date when the panel would be sitting again and would be able to hear my case, but was told that it would be at least for 6 months or maybe a bit longer before this happened. So it would just to be a waiting game until he was informed of the date and then passed the information on to me. In the meantime he would have to find out more about all the details about the breakup of my marriage and what had led up to it. So again I had to go into all the details that had happened and as most of his questions were of an intimate manner I felt so embarrassed at telling this man such personal things. He must have noticed my discomfort because he said that he was sorry about having to question me about my personal life but I had to understand that these were the questions that the panel would be asking me and I would have to be prepared to answer them.

When I told John what had happened he was sympathetic but said that it would all be worthwhile if at the end of it I would be free to marry, but to me *if* was the operative word as I could see by the way the lawyer spoke his feelings were like mine, and a happy ending was indeed a remote possibility. But I had started on this procedure so I would have to continue with it and only pray that there would be a successful conclusion. Having to wait for an answer for such a long time was going to be the hardest part of all. Six months passed and still no word from the lawyer, and I had begun to think that the waiting was never going to end. But then one day I received a letter from him to tell me that he had some news for me and that I should come to his office the

174

following week when he would give me the information that I had been waiting on for so long. When I went to his office the following week he informed that the panel would be sitting in six weeks time and I had to attend there at the appointed date. I was glad at least the waiting was over but I dreaded what was going to be the hardest part of facing a panel of strangers and answering their questions.

Chapter 16

While these events were happening in my personal life there were major changes going on the wider world. When Yuri Gagarin become the first man to orbit the earth in 1961 we were told that in a few years time that a man would be able to land on the surface of the moon and now this had happened. In the previous month, July 1969, Neil Armstrong of the USA joined by fellow astronaut Buzz Aldrin made history with the now famous words as he stepped on to the surface of the moon. 'That's one small step for a man, a giant leap for mankind'. People from all over the world watched and marvelled at what man's skill and ingenuity had accomplished, but in the midst of the celebrations there was also regret that with all the skill manpower plus millions of pounds that had gone into this project why couldn't some of this skill be used to alleviate the misery of drought, disease, hunger and poverty that beset so many of the inhabitants of the poorer countries of the world where life was a daily grind of misery and hardship. But it was always so, and as the saying goes, 'The rich get richer and the poor get babies and nothing changes'.

On a lighter note John and his oldest son has decided to change jobs and move to Corby where my brother Joe had told them that there were jobs available for them and the housing was now much easier to obtain as there was not such a long waiting list and that he would be willing to put them up until they were allocated a house of their own. So in November 1969 they set off with the promise of sending for John's family, myself and

Raymond as soon as they were settled down. John's daughter Mary was getting married in November and asked if she could stay with me until then, and Catherine and Charles who were also each in steady relationships, decided to stay on in the family home. So it was decided that was how it would be resolved.

The other members of my family were also on the move, Annie my oldest sister and her husband Jimmy had decided to move to Australia to stay with their daughter Rose who had moved there with her husband Tommy and their family a few years earlier and were now settled in their own home. As Annie was due to retire quite soon and Jimmy had already done so they decided to spend their retirement years with their family over there.

When John was in Corby he sent me a money order every week so that I could put it into the bank towards the time we would get a house of our own in Corby. He had stored most of his furniture in Jackie's bedroom as this was never used and Jackie had always slept in the bed in the kitchen since his father had died. John left only the necessities for the family in the house while he was away. Before he had gone, Jackie, John and I were in the habit of going to the Palace, which was a bingo hall and had a variety show also on a Friday evening, and Jackie and I continued going there after John was away. A few weeks later, I won £98 on my bingo card. I was over the moon as this was quite a tidy sum at this time and it would be a bumper addition to our savings, I gave £10 to Jackie and the same amount to Mary and James who were babysitting for me and were getting married the following month. Mary had already bought her wedding dress but as was typical of her, had omitted to buy herself a coat which she badly needed. So the money came in handy for that. As it was nearly Christmas I also sent money to John to buy something that he needed and Raymond got a new trench coat for the wet weather. The rest of the money went into the bank. Raymond's coat was not one of my better buys. It had a hood attached and the first time he wore it, one of his friends said it was a girl's coat because of the hood and afterwards it was battle of will getting him to wear it. I guess you can't win them all.

Winning this money had given my spirits a boost but the dread of appearing before that panel uppermost in my mind quite overshadowed my good fortune. The dreaded day arrived and I was shaking with nerves at the prospect before me. John was due to have two days off from work, so he insisted on taking me for the interview and said he would wait outside in the car until it was all over. This helped me quite a lot just to know that he would be there when it was finished.

The panel was sitting in a small hall with a large table down the centre. There were four of them and they were introduced as a priest, a lawyer, and a doctor, plus one who was there to record my answers to the questions that were asked of me. For almost two hours they delved into every aspect of my married life, including all the intimate details. When I mentioned that my brother-in-law was a priest, one of them asked me why I had not confided my problems to him. I told them that I had never even spoke of these to my closest family as I was too ashamed to admit that my marriage was a failure and especially not to Father Joe, as to him marriage was a sacred bond and should never be broken, so I did not think he would be very sympathetic to my problem. As I said, the questions went on for nearly two hours and sometimes the same one would be asked over again and I got the impression that they were trying to catch me out and were just checking that my answer was the same as the answer I had given them originally. When finally it was over I felt that I had been put through a wringer, and felt absolutely drained physically and emotionally. I was told that the findings would be passed to my lawyer in due course and I was informed that I was free to leave. When I arrived at the car and John looked at my face he said, 'My God, what has happened to you?'. I then promptly burst into tears. I hope that I never have to go through another experience like that again. I felt that I had been stripped naked and exposed to the world. My only hope now was that the outcome would prove to have been worth all the anguish. I had been warned that it would be a difficult process but I had never thought it would be so emotionally draining and would affect me so deeply.

In early February 1970 John wrote to tell me that he had been offered a house near the town centre and was so excited about it. As I was not able to go with him to see the property, Betty said that she would accompany him to give him a second opinion. But when they went to see it, their high hopes and expectations were soon dashed. The house was in a poor state of repair and the garden was like a junkyard. Betty was as disappointed as John and advised him not to accept it as she felt there must be something better and this would turn up soon. Betty was a school governor now and in this capacity she knew most of the councillors and promised John that she would find out about what could be done about better housing and when it would be available.

A couple of years before, the council had built houses in what was known as the Lincoln Estate. These houses were more modern, with a large kitchen-diner instead of the usual small kitchen. Yhey had a breakfast bar down the middle of the room which was ideal for a working surface and kept the usual clutter to a minimum. The trouble was that they were very difficult to obtain as most people were eager to have one and the numbers were very limited. We were offered one that had only been built two years previously and was situated in a street called Binbrook Walk. The council had requisitioned three of them for schoolteachers in that area, and these houses were numbered 6, 8 and 10. Betty had heard that a couple of teachers that were living there at the moment in number 8 had recently gained promotion and were moving away from the area, so she decided to speak to the councillor in the housing department on our behalf. Betty had worked tirelessly on his behalf when he was up for re-election to the council and I think he owed her a favour in return and this was his chance to repay her. So he agreed that we could move into number 8 when the present tenants had gone.

When John and Betty went to see it they were delighted to find that it lived up to more than their expectations. There were three bedrooms, two rather small but adequate and a larger one, a bathroom and a separate toilet and nice sized decent garden which was entirely enclosed and only accessible from the kitchen. I knew of course that of course we had only been fortunate enough to be given the tenancy because of Betty's intervention. I suppose some would say that this reeked of nepotism knowing someone who had the power to help when you needed them, but we were not going to split hairs. We were so grateful to Betty for her help and so pleased at our good fortune, so we did not query the decision. This was just one of the many times that Betty had come to my aid when I needed it most and I owe her a great debt of gratitude.

John came home for the weekend before the move and we, John, Raymond and I moved to Corby in February 1970. Young John, his wife Elizabeth and their family had been allocated a house a few weeks previously and were only staying a few minutes walk away from our house, so they made sure that everything was ready for us when we arrived as John had left them a spare key. Events however, did not go as planned. On the day we left there was a blizzard blowing and when we got over the border we missed our stopping at

Kettering station because we could not see the signs because of the snow, and the train continued all the way to London before we had realised our mistake. We were in a proper state of worry and confusion but there was nothing we could do about it until the train reached London. When we finally arrived there we told a porter what had happened and he informed us that there was a train leaving for Kettering from a different platform in a few minutes time, so we all rushed along to catch it, John with our luggage and me dragging Raymond along as fast I could. Thankfully we just made it in time and soon we were on the move again but of course in the opposite direction to that which we had intended. We duly arrived in Kettering and went from there to Corby. Two hours later than planned we finally arrived at the house. John and his wife were in a state of nerves thinking there must have been an accident to have held us up for so long, and of course we had no way of letting them know what had happened. There were no mobile phones in those days. But at least we had finally arrived safe and sound.

The wintery weather stayed with us for a few weeks longer, with the snow still laying on the ground and a bitterly cold wind blowing, but at least the house was lovely and warm. At least the kitchen and lounge were, but alas not the bedrooms which had no heating at all. We did not spend much time there except for sleeping and with plenty of bedding to try and keep the heat in us. The kitchen and lounge were heated by under floor heating which we discovered later was the most expensive kind. When we received our first heating bill it was for £225, a fortune to us. How were we going to pay such an enormous amount with only John's wages to depend on and so many things to be purchased for the house? The couple who had lived in the house previously, both school teachers, had taken everything portable with them before they left, even the electric light bulbs from every room.

Things were pretty hard financially for the first few months as there were no overtime at this time of the year and with the holiday period still to come there was no extra workers needed to fill in for anybody that was absent. It was getting so bad that John almost had to beg his overseer to get an extra shift to help out. It was now basic wages every week which was only £10 and there was so much that we needed for the house so there was no way we could manage on that amount.

There was only one way out of this and that was for me to get a job, Raymond was now settled in his new school and I felt that this was the right time for me to find out what was available on the job market. A few days later I was glancing at the local free paper and saw an advertisement for job vacancies in the Woolworths store in the town centre. So I went for an interview and did a small written test and was told to start the following week. I was sent to the makeup and jewellery department which pleased me very much, I felt it would be more interesting than most of the other departments as I was also interested in makeup and I felt that I could do a good job there. I soon settled into my new job and really enjoyed it. The shop was a very busy one as it was in the centre of the town and the staff were very friendly and helpful, so the days passed very quickly and I was enjoying the experience of being back at work again and of course enjoying the money also. The wages were £9.60 a week which was a great help financially and now we could start building up our home again.

There was a fund available in John's work which would pay the bills for bringing the furniture down from Glasgow to Corby for the people who were moving from there to work in the Steel Works and this money would be taken off the employee's wages every week until the bill was settled. We made use of this and applied for our belongings to be brought down to Corby. When the furniture arrived we discovered that nothing fitted in our new home. The carpets were either too large or too small for the rooms and the curtains were the same. Of course we needed new beds also and the furniture that John had stored in Jackie's room was now covered in a blue tinge as the room they had been stored in was unused and never heated and this led to the discolouration, John was very upset about his furniture as it had been highly glossed and of good quality and it took him months of polishing before he could restore it to his former glory but now at least we had something that we could start making our house into a home again and would have plenty of time to lick it into shape.

Jackie had been very upset when we told him of our move. He was used to having us nearby and spent a lot of time in our house and he was going to be very lonely when we were gone. I suggested that he had come down at the Easter weekend which was only a few weeks away and spend it with us in Corby and he jumped at the chance to do so. When he arrived he was delighted with the house and the town. There were plenty of nice walks round about and the scenery delighted him as we were so close to the country and nearby villages. He and Raymond could go for the long walks that they both enjoyed so much. When the weekend was over Jackie was loathe to leave. I knew he was dreading going back to an empty house after being used to being in company. John and I discussed this matter and decided to ask him to move down to stay with us if he wished to do so. We had the room now and he had nothing to keep him in Glasgow. When we told him he was overjoyed and said he would go back in and put in his notice at work and come to Corby at the Glasgow Fair Holiday in July, but after a few weeks at home he wrote to tell us that he could not wait until then and had given in his notice and would be with us in a couple of weeks time. That was no problem to us as he was no bother to look after and he would be good company for Raymond, as he though the world of his 'Unc' as he called him. And so it was agreed. His original weekend holiday became a period of almost twenty five years as he stayed with us until he died in 1995, aged 80 years old.

We had now been settled in our new home for eight months and everything was going well. The house was taking shape and I was enjoying my job. There was still no word from my lawyer but I had been warned about the length of time an annulment could take so I knew I would just have to be patient and hope that no news would be a good sign and maybe suggest a successful outcome. I had informed my lawyer of my change of address when I had moved to Corby, so it was just a matter of time now playing the waiting game. As it happened I did not have to wait for very much longer as a few weeks later I heard from Ross Harper that I had won my case and my annulment and I would receive official authorisation of this in due course. He also said that he would now be able to begin the divorce proceedings and that he would keep me informed on how matters were progressing. I had given him the only address I knew of where my husband might be staying and that was at his parent's house in Lambhill. Again I settled in for a long wait but a month later the lawyer wrote again to say that he had tried to find this address in order to serve the divorce papers but found that the house and surrounding buildings had been demolished a few years earlier and there was now no way of locating where the tenants had moved to so the papers could not be served. The divorce case had to be held in Edinburgh High Court the following month and with no one there to contest the case the divorce was granted automatically. As soon I was informed of this I went to see my parish priest, Father Fennel, and explained my situation to him. I thought that he might be a bit offhand with me, knowing the Church's feelings about divorce, but he was very kind and understanding and said that as long as he received the authorisation of the annulment of the marriage he would be happy to marry us in his church. He pencilled in the date of the 7th December 1970 which was only a few weeks away. I left feeling happier than I had when I arrived, and just hoping that the finalities would be sorted out in time and that at last the wedding would be finalised. The official forms were received a few days later and I took them immediately to Father Fennel. Now everything was ready for our wedding day, but mixed with the feelings of relief and happiness there was a deep feeling of regret and sadness. I had started on my seventeen years of married life full of youthful high hopes and the certainty that this was the beginning of a life with an ending of happy ever after, but unfortunately this was not be realised and now that seventeen years had been wiped out in a few minutes in the confines of a cold and austere court with the words, 'divorce granted', as if these years had never been. There were no victors in this battle, only sadness at the waste of our two lives and regrets for what might have been.

There was now a race on to sort out the wedding arrangements, John had written to his oldest brother Michael in Manchester to ask him if he would agree to be his best man and he readily agreed to do so, I had been in touch with Chris to ask her to be my bridesmaid and she said that she would be delighted to do so. She was now staying in Scotland but said she would travel down in time for the wedding. Naturally we did not want a big fuss made as it was a second marriage for both of us, but we had to mark our special day with some form of celebration. John and I were in the habit of having lunch in a pleasant restaurant in Kettering when we were shopping in that area and we got to know the owners very well, so John asked them if we could have the dining room for lunch for our guests on our wedding day and they readily agreed. We then ordered taxis to take our bridal party from the church to the restaurant and we also intended to have a little party for other friends and relations at our house in the evening.

The day of the wedding 7th December dawned dry and bright but bitterly cold and the church was absolutely freezing. I was so glad that I had put my fur coat which John had given me previously in the back of the car as everyone else was shivering while we stood getting the wedding photograph's taken. I wore a dress and matching coat and John had on his dinner suit, so I think we looked quite smart on our special day.

There were quite a few people at the lunch; John and I, Chris and her husband, Michael and his wife, Betty and Joe, Jackie and Raymond, John and Liz and John and Marie. John and Liz had their two children with them and John and Marie had their four children with them also. There was also one unseen and uninvited guest, John and Liz's third child who was expected any day and had Liz in a panic for days beforehand wondering if it would arrive in time for her to be able to attend the wedding. Thankfully the baby did not arrive until the 11th December, four days after the wedding, and they named their only daughter Elaine. Altogether we had quite a happy band at lunch. In fact, altogether we had a really lovely day and everyone seemed to enjoy themselves. John and I gave ourselves a pat on the back as everything we had put together in such a short space of time had turned out so well.

I had started to work in Woolworth's in April 1970 and our currency was due to be changed to decimalisation on February 15th 1971. It was to be a mammoth change for the public and the staff to get used to this new money. The staff had to have lessons in dealing with the change over so we could answer any queries from the public. Every week we went for a half

186

hour's lesson in the canteen.This went on for a few months before the change over until we were fully conversant with the news system. We had always been used to counting our money in blocks of twelve. There were 12 pennies in a shilling and 240 pennies in a pound, but with this new system there was 5 new pence to a shilling and a hundred new pence to the pound. This was to bring us into line with the other continental countries who counted their money in units of ten instead of twelve as we had normally done originally. The British public were entirely confused with this system and the older people kept trying to convert the new coinage back to what they were used to which made it very difficult for them, so eventually it was decided by some bright spark at head office that each item on the shop counter had to have two prices on display, one with the pre-decimal price and the other with the new decimal price of the cost of the goods. These had to be on show for a few weeks until hopefully the customer became more used to this new system. This of course made a lot of extra work for the staff and although it was supposed to help the public understand the money I think personally it confused them even more. The most asked question at that time was, 'But how much is that in real money?'.

We were also told that the notes we were used to were being phased out. We were originally familiar with a ten shilling note and pound note; now they were introducing a 50 pence coin instead of the ten shillings and a pound coin instead of the pound note. The public moaned and grumbled about having to carry so many heavy coins in their pockets and purses but accepted the inevitable. Not so in Scotland where the people refused to deal with the one pound coin and demanded the paper money instead. This bloodless revolution went on for a few months until the notes were almost unusable and had become so thin and dirty with constant usage, and as there was no more new ones being issued they eventually had to accept that this hated coin was here to stay and there was nothing to do but accept it. On the other side of the coin, no pun intended, was the realisation of the fact that we were now paying almost double the price for goods than we had previously, and this had almost gone unnoticed in all the confusion and it was only now that people had realised what had occurred.

Chapter 17

The 70's were good years for us. We loved our house and John and I were both happy in our jobs and Raymond had settled well in his new school. We also had become good friends with our neighbours at number 6, young John and his wife. He taught at the local school and she worked at the labour exchange in town. They had no family but had a lovely dog as a pet named Shandy which she had got from the local animal shelter. It was 90% Labrador and a beautiful animal with a gentle nature and very friendly. Young John would call in everyday after school with the dog and take Raymond for long walks with them. I had no experience at all of dogs; we had always had a cat when I was younger as in the old tenement buildings there was plenty of places for the mice to breed and most households had a cat to keep their numbers in check, but none of our immediate neighbours had dogs.

John had a dog, Glen, before I knew him but it had to be put down shortly before we left because of a leg infection, but John still missed him very much and envied his neighbour his beautiful pet. When he mentioned this to young John he said that he would take him to the same animal shelter where he had got his dog to see if he could see any animal that he would like to take home with him. A few days later we had another addition to our family who was named Brandy, a lovely bitch mostly labrador as well. John was delighted with his new pet and the two dogs soon became great friends and played together happily in our garden. When young John went off to school in the morning he would tether

Shandy to the garden fence with a long lead so it could move about freely, but had no sooner had he gone off than Shandy would come to our end of the fence and start digging with her paws to make a large hole, Brandy would do the same thing at our end and before long there would be enough of a gap for Shandy to slither through to our garden and there she would stay for the rest of the day playing happily with Brandy until her owner came back from school to pick him up. The first time that this happened he was amazed to find his dog in our garden instead of his own, but after this happened day after day we told him not to bother tying his dog up in the morning as the dogs had made their own escape tunnel and were intending to use it in future, so we just left them to do their own thing.

This went on for a few months until young John got a promotion to Lancaster. We missed our good neighbours and Brandy was pining for her friend. She had never wandered away from home before but suddenly she would go missing for a few days on end until eventually she did not return. John said that she had probably gone to find Sandy and probably been picked up by someone who had given her a new home. We never did find out what happened to her but we missed her dreadfully and only hoped that where ever she was she was well looked after and happy.

When John lived in Glasgow he only had a small plot in the back garden in which he mostly grew vegetables and some flowers, but now that he had a decent sized piece of land he was able to plant a lot more and could give in to his passion for his favourite flowers which were roses. He trained a rose bush to grow up on the outside wall over our bedroom windows and when it came into bloom it was a site to behold. Strangers used to stop and take photographs and one of our neighbours who being a very keen photographer had sent the photograph of the rose bush into the local paper and they published it. Those were very happy days and to make it even better I now had most of my family living nearby. Annie and Jimmy had come home from Australia as Annie had never really settled there, although they both had jobs and were doing well but Annie was very homesick, so they returned after two years. John and Marie had also moved down to Corby so the Dawson clan was starting to gather strength. Peter came down for the occasional weekend and always spent his two weeks annual holiday with Joe and Betty, so we did not lose touch with him either. Jackie had also settled in well and was working as a washroom attendant in the Steel Works. It was not strenuous work, just a matter of keeping the men supplied with soap, towels etc. and keeping the place clean, so it suited him very well.

In the 1970's there were many happy sunshine filled days, but behind the sun and not yet visible the dark stormy clouds were gathering. There was to be a new steel works plant at Redcar which was to be used to make steel and would take the place of Corby with all future orders being processed there, so making the town of Corby redundant with the loss of 6,000 jobs. The union immediately called for a strike which was to begin immediately and lasted for thirteen weeks. The people in Corby could not believe what was happening to them and their town; Stewart and Lloyds was Corby and without it we had nothing to take its place and people were already muttering about it going to be a ghost town. The strike only ended when the men were forced to return when the management announced that unless the men returned to work immediately there was to be no redundancy paid. After thirteen weeks nothing had been achieved by the strike except the loss of three months wages. The works eventually closed down in April 1980 and with that the heart was torn out of Corby and the future seemed very bleak. However, in April

1981 Corby was made an Enterprise Zone to try and attract some employment into the town. Any employer who took up the challenge was promised a twoyear free rental as an inducement and slowly a few small premises were opened up and then some larger firms like RS Components also took up the challenge. Gradually we started to hope that perhaps Corby would weather the storm. Of course some of the smaller firms did leave after the two years but some did some prosper and stayed here, and slowly we were climbing the ladder again. Personally during the strike we were in a better position than most of the families here as I was working and John had been on the sick pay after a bad bout of the flu, so at least we were having something coming in, whereas households with only one worker were finding things really difficult.

The men in the Steel Plant were offered counselling with regards to their redundancy money. There were two alternatives; they could either take a lower amount of redundancy and a lifelong pension, or a larger redundancy and no pension. John took the lower redundancy payment and the pension which seemed the wiser choice at the time. The pension aged started at 55 or over and John again was very fortunate, he had just celebrated his 54th birthday but they gave him a few months more work to bring him up to the required age for the pension.

In the meantime Raymond had sat his A-Level exams. He had always wanted to go to university if he got the required marks that he needed, and he had applied to St. Andrews and was taking Latin, English and History for his subjects. There was no other student in Corby taking Latin so he was lucky in the fact that he was given one-to-one tuition. He passed his exams and left for university in October 1980. A few weeks later the prizes for the exams in his old school had to be given out but as Raymond was not able to attend John and I went in his place. When the first prize for English was announced Raymond had come top of his class and John went up to the stage to receive his prize. The man who was handing out prizes looked at him, 15 stone, five foot ten in height and said, 'My God, you are a big lad aren't you?'. The audience laughed but I felt sorry for John. When this happened four more times he said, 'I am not going up there again, you can go in my place'. Thankfully it did not happen again because the joke was wearing a bit thin and John was getting a bit fed up. A few year's later, the day of Raymond's university graduation was the proudest day of our lives. When we saw him going up on the stage with his cap and gown to receive his certificate even John and Jackie had tears in their eyes and I thought to myself, 'Who would have thought that from such a lowly start things would have turned out so well?'.

I seemed to have got a bit ahead of myself, so I will retrace my steps a little. We had been in Corby now for a few years, but had never been on holiday yet as a family unit. Now we decided that things had settled down that this was as good a time as any and as we had saved up a bit of money we felt that we now earned a break and started to look in the holiday section of the papers for a suitable place to go to. There was an advertisement for a holiday for a farm in Cornwall and we all quite liked the idea of staying on a farm and as none of us had been to Cornwall before we thought it would be something totally different from our usual type of holiday. John wrote immediately and booked a week's holiday there. Raymond was now a teenager and we knew that he would soon get bored with only his parents for company so we decided to ask his cousin Jeremy, my sister Chris's son, to come with us. There was not much difference in their ages and they seemed to get on quite well together and we thought this would be quite a good idea and Jeremy was delighted to come.

The farm was in a little village called Kirkhampton which was on the border between Devon and Cornwall and it was called Haywood farm. John hired a car and we set off with John, myself, Raymond, Jeremy and Jackie on board. It was about an eight hour drive, so we decided to stop about halfway to break the journey and give John a chance to recover as he was the only driver. Halfway to our destination we found a little cottage which had a vacancy so we stopped there for the night. It was actually two cottages made into one and the rooms were very cute with sloping roofs and you could step right into the garden from the room. The boys loved it.

The next morning we drove into Kilkhampton and John stopped a passerby for directions to the farm. We were told to carry on up the road we were on until we came to a branch off with some lanes leading off from it, and to turn off at the one that had four milk churns at the bottom, and that we would find the farm at the top of that lane. Not the usual kind of instructions you expect to receive, but we followed the directions which were given and drove on, keeping our eyes peeled for the milk churns, where we turned off and drove up to the top and came to a huddle of dilapidated old sheds. We looked at one another with horror and disbelief. Surely we had not been intended to live here. There was nobody around to ask, so we waited for a few minutes and had just decided to turn back when we saw a woman running towards us. She stopped at the car and asked us who we were looking for and when we told her Haywood's Farm, she laughed and said you have not come up far enough. This is where we keep the farm implements; the farm is just a little bit further up the lane. Well thank goodness for that, I thought. We followed her up the road and came to the farm and what a change. It was quite an old building but there was a lovely garden with a swing and a hammock and the farm was in the background. The lady introduced herself as Mrs. Haywood and invited us into the house. It was a typical farm house with a very large kitchen and dining room both with stone flooring and with the bedrooms upstairs. When she showed us our room I was delighted with it. There was a lovely old fashioned dressing table with a set of drawers and a wardrobe to match and all spotlessly clean, and on the bed a beautiful lace bed cover. When I remarked on this she told me that it had been her grandmother's and wa about a hundred years old. I told her that I was surprised that such a precious thing was being used in a holiday guest's bedroom but she explained that she only took one family at a time and most of her guests came back year after year and she knew that they would take care of her possessions.

Next morning when we came down for breakfast I could understand why people kept coming back year after year. On the table was about six packets of different cereals and three large platters of food, one with bacon and sausages and another with about half a dozen fried eggs and still another with a heap of fried potatoes. I had never seen so much food in my life and as we trooped into the room she appeared with two racks of toast and two large pots of tea, one for each side of the table. We ate until we were really full but there was still an awful lot of food left when we had finished. I thought what a waste of such lovely food but John said that probably the family ate it after we were finished.

At dinner that night there was another feast with the addition of dessert; two large cakes, one sponge and one meringue, and both served with Cornish cream. I could not imagine that this kind of culinary perfection could last all week but it did. I must have gained about a stone in weight and Jeremy looked as though he has swallowed a football. The family consisted of Mr and Mrs Haywood, their son Peter, his wife and their two children, a boy about two years of age and a baby girl. Their other son had a small farm of his own. Mr

Haywood was a typical farmer in looks with a ruddy complexion and rather rough in manner, but his wife was entirely different, rather petite and very gentile, but then, as they say, opposites attract. Peter's wife was small and thin but she worked as hard as the med did on the farm from morning till night, while the baby lay in a battered old pram in the yard where her mother could keep her eyes on it while she went about her work. It was not an easy life but they seemed happy enough with their lot. Tina the little girl soon attached herself to us and we would take her with us when we went out which gave her mother a break and I know she was very grateful for that.

As I said before Kirkhampton lay between Devon and Cornwall and each morning we would look to the bottom of the lane and look in each direction to see where the sun was shining brightest and we would head in that direction to spend our day. If it was Devon we would go to Westward Ho, which was a holiday resort, and we had found a little cafe there where they served delicious hot doughnuts with coffee and we would have a walk along the beach afterwards and try out luck at the different amusement stalls. If it was Cornwall we would go and watch the men fishing for shrimps or we would visit Tintagel where there was an old castle which according to folklore had been used by King Arthur and his Knights in days gone by, or we would explore the little coves where the smugglers used to hide their boats. The boys loved to explore all these places and never seemed to get bored. Jeremy was hoping to go to university eventually to study Geography which was his favourite subject.

There was a little stream that ran through the farm and Jeremy decided that he would find out where it had its source, so one morning he set out with Raymond tagging along as usual in his wake. It had rained heavily the night before and the ground was still very wet and muddy, Raymond stepped into a large puddle and sank to his knees in mud. He struggled to get out and lost his shoe in the process and was covered in mud from his feet to his knees. It was almost a week before the farmer found his shoe and of course it was unwearable and caked in muck and dirt. I had bought him the new shoes and denims before we left on holiday and now both these articles were ruined. I told Jeremy if he wanted to find out where the river started that he should do the right thing and go to Egypt and search out the source of the Nile and leave the little farm's stream alone in the future.

Since the time of The Beatles in the 60's followed by the Flower People whose slogan was 'Make Love Not War', teenagers had changed out of all recognition in their dress, their vocabulary and even their choice of music. Raymond was no exception to the rule. He had let his hair grown almost to his shoulders and when I looked at him I could hardly recognise him from the person he used to be. He became quite moody and was keen on heavy rock music which drove us mad and almost deafened us. Even the word teenager was something new to us. When we were that age we were seen but definitely not heard but now a whole new culture had grown up around them in their fashion and their speech and their music. The world that we knew was changing and not for the better and the innocence of children and childhood had gone forever. Now they were seen and most definitely heard and now the world belonged to them.Thankfully in Raymond's case the change was fleeting and he soon went back to his normal ways except for the long hair and the love of heavy rock music which lasted for a few more years.

In 1975 young John and his Family emigrated to Canada to start a new life. Elizabeth his wife already had two aunts living there and they kept telling her what a marvellous country it was and full of opportunities for young people, so finally they decided that the time was right to make the move. John drove them to the airport and was really upset at their departure and wondering if he would ever see them again. They settled in a little place called Thornhill in Ontario which was about an hour's drive from Toronto and soon found jobs. John has served his apprenticeship as a butcher and now worked in a large store in the meat department. Elizabeth had a few part time jobs at the beginning but eventually got a full time job in the pharmacy department of the local hospital. After a few months they managed to rent a flat and settled down to enjoy their new lives, while at home John and I started to save for the trip to Canada to visit them.

Raymond was now 14 years of age and started at the local secondary school, Pope John's. In the junior school that he had attended previously, Our Lady's, the teachers were very strict and the pupils had to work very hard at their studies, but when he moved to his new school he found that things were much more relaxed and the teachers not nearly so strict as at the previous school. In fact, there was a standing joke among the pupils that they had moved from Belsen to Butlins.

Raymond always wanted to learn to play the piano but we did not have one at home and although there was quite a few music teachers in Corby who taught piano they did not take pupils unless they had the instrument at home so that they could practice what they had been taught. As luck would have it, one of my friend's at work Lilly had a son, now married, who used to go for lessons but had lost interest. His piano was still in the house with nobody there to play it so she offered it to me. I insisted on paying something for it but she would only accept a very small sum. Raymond got his piano and now had been taking lessons for a couple of years and doing very well. We looked after it and had it tuned regularly and Raymond had it for years afterwards, I thought he would get very bored after a time but he kept going to lessons until he was almost 16 years of age, taking his yearly exams until he reached grade 5 and was a very proficient player. He played at different locations for a fee after we had bought him a portable electric piano that he could carry around. He also taught himself the guitar, so that gave him a second string to his bow.

Chapter 18

Things were moving along very nicely for us but life never runs smoothly for long and in July 1978 a tragedy struck our family when it was least expected. As I said before my brother Joe used to spend his yearly holiday with Peter as he intended to do that year but when he arrived at the house a neighbour told him that Peter had been taken to hospital the previous day with what they thought was a severe case of flu and Joe went down there immediately to see him. Peter gave him his wallet and gold watch that he had been awarded for long service at work a few years previously and had brought them from the house for safe keeping. He asked Joe to keep them safe for him until he came home but when Joe spoke to the doctor in charge he was told that Peter had leukaemia and not flu and needed bone marrow. Joe offered immediately to be a donor and he was told to come back the following morning for tests to see if he was suitable. Joe went home with a very heavy heart hardly believing what was happening. When he returned the following morning to the hospital he was told that Peter had died unexpectedly in the early hours of the morning. Joe was devastated. He had come to spend a holiday with Peter but now instead of that he had to make plans for his funeral. He phoned Betty to ask her to break the news to the family. When she did we were totally disbelieving. How could this happen so quickly and without any warning when we had not even known he was ill? He was only 51 years of age and we just could not believe what had happened. It was a nightmare but one that we would not wake up from. Peter had led a rather lonely life since my mother had died. Most of his friends had married and had families of their own and although Peter had a few girlfriends over the years there was no permanent relationship which evolved from there, so he remained a bachelor. It was a sad and lonely life and he deserved so much more.

Joe had arranged the date of the funeral for the following Tuesday which only gave us a couple of days to settle everything in Corby before we travelled to Glasgow. There was no time to clear out the house so everything had to be left as it was. We each took a small memento but all the furniture had to remain. Peter had bought for himself a large leather armchair a few years previously which was his pride and joy and we did not want to leave that to strangers. So we managed to find a firm to take it to Walsall to my sister Chris's house as she was the only one who had the space to fit it in, but everything else was left the way it was.

On the day of the funeral it was bright and warm and somehow that made things even harder for us. Most people were out enjoying the summer day and we were burying my brother and it just seemed so wrong. There was quite a good turnout at his funeral. A bus had been laid on by his employers to take his workmates to the funeral as a mark of respect, and there was also quite a few of our friends who had heard about his death and also my old friend Nora. It was nice to sit and talk to her again even although it had taken a funeral to bring us together. The family had to travel back to Corby the same night as we had to be at work the following day. It was a very miserable journey home and now we had severed the last link with Glasgow. Life slowly got back to normal, although it was never the same as it had been before; another link in the family chain had been broken.

As I said before my Sister Annie had a very forceful personality and she was very intelligent and very confident in her own ability in getting things done. I looked up to her to and admired her good qualities but we had never really been very close as there was too many years in age between us. As she was now back in Corby after her two years away in Australia I invited her and Jimmy for lunch one Sunday and after we had our meal the men went into the lounge to watch a football match on the television and we were on our own. We started to talk about the family and the way things used to be when we were younger and as I listened to her I realised I did not really know my sister at all. I had always been a bit of a dreamer and Annie was the doer, but when she spoke I realised that although she put up a good facade I found that beneath the confident exterior she was as full of doubts and insecurities in just the same way as I was, and I realised how little we know of the person underneath the front that they are hiding behind, and for the first time I felt really close to my sister. We spoke for hours quite undisturbed and when she left that evening she said that it had been the nicest day that she had spent in years and I felt the same thing.

A few weeks later she had a few chest pains and went to see her doctor who told her that her heart was not very sound and that she would have to take things a lot easier and rest more than she did. A few years earlier she had been diagnosed with diabetes and been given a diet sheet which meant that she had to deny herself all the sweet things like cakes and chocolates which she was so fond of and if this did not work she would have to have injections. She stuck rigidly to the diet and lost quite a few stone in weight and looked years younger as a result. She looked really attractive and began to dress more stylishly and that of course improved her appearance. I was pleased for her as I knew that she was dreading to have the injections but now this would not be necessary. This relief was very short lived as she continued to have chest pains and in March 1979 she had a heart attack and died at 68 years of age, less than a year after we had lost Peter.

I could not believe that Annie had gone from our lives. To me she had always seemed invincible and would go on forever. The trouble was that she did not know the meaning of taking things easy and always had to be busy; her hands were never idle and to make matters worse she was a perfectionist in everything she did. Everything had to be done properly with no cutting of corners and if she was not busy with housework she would be knitting or sewing, anything that would keep her active because to her idleness was a cardinal sin and must be avoided at all cost. But the body is only a machine and eventually it runs down and Annie had worked hers to a standstill.

My brother John and his wife Marie had settled down well in Corby. John was working in the boiler room at Avon which was a large cosmetic factory and seemed very happy there. At Christmas the staff got the chance to but the merchandise at a bargain price and much to my surprise he had bought me a box of assorted make up as a Christmas present. There was everything in it, lipstick, eye shadow, powder etc. The only trouble was that when I applied it my skin came out in blotches as it was very highly perfumed and my skin was too sensitive for it, and the only item I could use was the shampoo. Of course I did not mention this to John as I really appreciated the gesture and anyhow it is the thought that counts. John's family were all growing up and he was a very proud father of four, two boys and two girls, Anna Marie, Silvio, Marco and Amanda, all Italian names that Marie had chosen and John was quite happy to go along with her choice. John was quite a strict father especially with the girls, but they were really a very devoted family and John was very much the head of it. He had always been a very active person and always appeared to be in the best of health so we were all very surprised when we discovered that he had a heart problem as we had never known him to be ill. On the 21ˢᵗ of May 1980 his daughter came home from school and, looking for her father, at first could not find him. Eventually she found him in the lounge sitting in his chair and thinking he was sleeping she tried to awaken him but to no avail. He had died from a sudden heart attack while sitting there; it was a peaceful way for him to go but a dreadful shock to all his family and especially to his daughter who had found him. So in three short years we had lost three of our family in sudden deaths.

It was a dreadful day when John was laid to rest, unknown to us he had stipulated in his will that he had wished a piper to play at his funeral and the family had agreed to this request. As our family were getting ready to follow the cortege the piper suddenly appeared and started to play The Flowers of the Forest and went to the head of the funeral precession to play us into the cemetery. I was walking beside Silvio and I could feel him trembling with grief. He was only a young lad and my heart ached for him, so I took his hand and held it tightly and he clung to me for the rest of the service. When they put the coffin into the ground Marie was crying uncontrollably and screaming, 'John, John'. I tried to comfort her but it was useless; she was half-leaning over the grave and I was terrified that she might fall in, so in a few minutes we had to lead her forcibly away. I knew how she must have been feeling; she was in a strange country without any of her own family to comfort her and now John whom she had depended on for everything was gone and she must have felt entirely alone. John was only 58 years of age and that was far too young to die, but at least he had many happy years with the family around him, so we to console ourselves with that thought. My biggest worry was about Marie and how she would cope without John. He had done everything for her, all the little things of everyday life; he did all the shopping, paid the bills and attended to all the household business and kept things running smoothly in the home. Although Marie had become quite good with the language and could speak it and understand it reasonably well she still lacked confidence in herself. As it happened Silvio took over. He visited her every night after work to make sure she was alright and helped her in every way, and slowly she took up the reigns again with his help.

We had been saving hard over the last few years so as we would be able to go to Canada and see John, Elizabeth and the grandchildren and after the heartbreak of losing the members of my family I felt that now was the right time to go as they were both settled in a new country and had their new house and had the space to accommodate us as well. As it happened however, it was an unfortunate time for us to go as a few days before our flight was due the air traffic controllers of Toronto Airport went on strike and were not receiving any planes to that airport. We were forced to go on a diversion to Buffalo in America and then to be taken by bus into Toronto. It was a dreadful journey as there was turbulence throughout the whole of the flight and we had to keep our seatbelts fastened all the time we were on the plane. It was even harder for John as this was the first time for him being in a plane and he was in a nervous state before we even started the journey but now there was an added anxiety not knowing when or if we would reach Toronto as the pilot announced that due to the weather we might have to land somewhere different from the original planned destination.

We had set off at 6am in the morning and it was now evening and we still had not received permission to land anywhere. Finally at 6pm we were told that we would have to go to a hotel overnight and wait there till the weather started to clear. At the hotel we were given dinner and allocated a room for the night but we could not settle to sleep so we just had a shower and lay on top of the bed. At 4am we received a phone call to our room to say that we had to go immediately for the plane which would be taking off for Buffalo very soon. When we did land at Buffalo we were informed that the bus would arrive soon to take us the rest of our journey. It was now 7am and it was becoming unbearably hot and as the plane was on the ground all the air conditioning was turned off and we sat there with the perspiration running down our faces and praying that the bus would arrive soon so that we could get out of the plane which was now like an oven. Eventually it did arrive and what bliss; it was air-conditioned and at last we could breathe again. We were then taken by bus to the airport at Toronto and at last we were able to meet the family more than thirty hours after we had left Britain on a journey that normally took about eight hours. The family were as relieved as we were as they had been phoning the airport every hour to find out if the bus arrived. We were all in tears of relief and, on our part, total exhaustion.

After a good night's sleep we were ready to go sightseeing. John and Elizabeth had arranged for us to go to Niagara Falls as we had heard so much about the place and eager to see if it was as wonderful as the pictures we had seen. When we got there we were issued with long raincoats which covered us from head to foot and large southwester hats which protected our head and our shoulders. We set out in a boat called the Maid of The Mist and soon reached the falls and what an awesome sight it was. There were tons of water crashing down from the rocks and the noise was vibrating like thunder in our ears. The boat went in as close as possible to the bottom of the falls and we were soon drenched and very glad of our protective clothing. It was an awesome feeling sitting in that boat and feeling as if we were alone in a world of water but the magic was not over yet as when we returned to land and had our meal we were informed that evening to see an even more glorious spectacle. When the darkness started to fall the falls were flood lit and we would be able to see them from the shore. About 9pm a light appeared and in a few seconds the falls were transfigured into a fairy land of dancing waters in colours of blue, green, orange and indigo. Words alone cannot describe the spectacle on which we gazed with delight and wonder. We have been back to Niagara a few times since but nothing could replace the magic of the first time we saw this wondrous sight of nature in all its splendour. A few days later we were taken to the Blue Mountain where you travelled to the top in a type of ski lift and if you were feeling adventurous could hire a sledge to whizz back down again. Elizabeth and I were quite willing to go on the ski lift but not too sure about the sledge. While we were debating about what course to take and with the two Johns jeering at us and saying we were cowards, suddenly a sledge passed us on its way down with two ladies of very mature age as its occupants and that settled the issue; if they could do it then we could to, so off we went whizzing round the corners and nothing between us and a sheer drop but a little brake on the sledge which you could use to slow down or stop. It was quite exciting on the descent but I for one was very glad to be on terra firma once again. On another day of our visit we went to the CN Tower - Canada National Tower - which was over 1,700 feet high and supposedly the highest free standing building in the world. When you reached the top there was a panoramic view of the city of Toronto, another marvellous sight.

Canada was a beautiful country, unlike its neighbour America, a melting pot of different nationalities and cultures but so different in many other ways. Life was so much slower and less frantic and everyone seemed to live quite happily side by side. We had gone over the border to America a few times and on one of our trips our destination was Florida, the Sunshine State and home to one of its greatest attractions, Disney World. I had always thought of it mainly for children but I was wrong; there was plenty for adults to see and enjoy, like Main Street where you could see life as it used to be lived with horses plodding along and all the old grey stone buildings that had been there long before skyscrapers had ever been thought of. Every year hundreds of students were employed to work and the place was kept spotlessly clean with never a sign of litter anywhere even though there were thousands of visitors coming every day. There was even a person employed to follow the horses to ensure that there were no accidents like the call of nature and if there was there, was no evidence of it left to offend the visitors. We went to visit the Hall of Presidents where the actors who played the parts were so like the originals it was absolutely uncanny. There was a beautiful building called the Magic Castle where Prince Charming and his Princess lived and this building was almost entirely made of glass and was a wonderful sight. Every year there was two students chosen to play these parts. The Prince was also very handsome and the Princess, of course, was beautiful. We and quite a few others had breakfast with them in the castle and they both were charming young people. Every night when dusk fell there was floodlight procession of floats carrying all the fairy tale characters and the look of awe and wonder on the children's faces as their favourites passed them smiling and waving was a joy to behold and even the older ones like ourselves were carried away at the wonderful spectacle happening before our eyes.

In the 17th Century a group of Indians called the Hurons settled in Canada in a place called Huronia and were later followed by missionaries who came to spread the word and teachings of the Christian faith. These two groups worked side by side and together they helped to build the church, St Marie, in the grounds of the settlement. Word soon spread about this new religion and people flocked to the St. Marie church to learn of this faith and practise it. Some if the converts became missionaries themselves and these continued to spread the Gospel to the people. Of course not all of the people agreed with the teachings of this new religion and nine missionaries were martyred for their faith and some of them are buried in the Martyr Shrine. These people were canonised in 1930 and made secondary patrons of Canada in 1940. In this beautiful place there were many lakes and gardens and statues of the different saints were everywhere. In the garden of Our Lady there is a replica of a pair of rosary beads comprised of coloured stones and supposedly copied from a pair of rosary beads found here 350 years ago. The Hurons left behind a legacy of faith in letters that had lain buried for centuries covered by over grown trees and shrubbery. The letters revealed the vibrant faith of the Hurons and the zeal of the missionaries who converted them. There is a path that is called the Way of the Cross, where visitors can trace the footsteps of Christ carrying his cross and these are entirely composed of rock that has been hewn out of the hillside. There is an aura of peace and tranquillity that fills the air and stays with you as you walk around. In the church hundreds of candles are burning as each pilgrim is expected to light one in memory of their visit to the shrine. It was another marvellous experience to add to all the others that we had witnessed in the beautiful country of Canada, and we give our grateful thanks to John and Elizabeth for sharing them with us.

There are still many signs of the Indian occupation around everywhere in Canada, in exotic names of places and in the little shops that spring up in the most unlikely places selling all kinds of Indian art objects. As I said, there are all kinds of nationalities here and a large proportion of them are from Scottish descent. On our way home after one of our visits we shared a seat on the plane with an emigrant who had left Scotland over 30 years before to settle in Canada. He belonged to a club called the Caledonians and every year they paid a visit home, and to them Scotland meant home. Although they had prospered in their new country they were inordinately very proud of their Scottish Heritage.

Canada is a land with many lakes. They have different cruises to go round the lakes; all day cruises, lunch ones and dinner cruises in the evening. And what could be nicer than sitting eating a meal and listening to the sparkling water lapping the side of the boat? We sampled all of these trips but my favourite one was the all-day one where we were piped aboard and had nothing to do all day but sit and admire the scenery with everything laid on for your comfort and wellbeing. Saying that, the dinner cruise came a very close second and after a glorious day of sunshine you could sit and watch the red ball of fire slowly sinking behind the water. Memories are usually made of these moments.

Chapter 19

In the early 80's Joe was having recurring problems with his throat and within a few months he could barely speak above a whisper, and eventually with persuasion from Betty he went to see his doctor and was horrified to be told that he had throat cancer, the same as my father had had. He lost weight very rapidly and was only a shadow of himself. He was taken to hospital for tests where they found that the cancer was well advanced and incurable. Afterwards he was in and out of hospital quite a few times in the following months as he was in a lot of pain, but there was nothing much to do to help him. A few times he was so ill that we thought we were going to lose him, but each time he rallied again and fought back to life. Although he was suffering so much he never lost his sense of humour and he even joked that he had more needles put into him than there were in a Singer sewing machine. When he was in hospital Betty would go and visit him every day. For the afternoon and evening, to give her a break, John suggested that he and I should go in for a change. I don't think she was very keen to do this as she felt she had to be there all the time with him, but eventually we talked her round and she agreed.

At this time the doctors had decided to remove his voice box and to do this they had to make an insertion in his throat and put a tube from the hole they had made into his stomach. They were trying to teach him to speak from his stomach but his words were very hard to understand and garbled; this was a difficult thing for him to learn to do. As he was now unable to speak properly, he had to write everything down when he wished to say something. I think this is the time when Joe gave up his brave fight for life as when he lost his voice he also lost his dignity.

On the night that John and I visited him he had his note paper and his pen already on the bedside table, he wrote down what he wanted to say to us and we had to reply the same way. To think that my handsome, clever brother had been reduced to this brought the tears to my eyes but I daren't cry as it would only have made things worse for him. Suddenly he put his hand towards me and I thought he wanted to write something down but John who was more perceptive than I was told me that he wanted to hold my hand. As I said before we were not a very tactile family and this surprised me but I did take his hand and he grasped it tightly and smiled at me. A short time later he suddenly took a turn for the worse and John went to find the nurse. She asked us if we would wait in another room until she called the doctor. John decided to phone Betty as he knew something was very wrong and Betty said she would come immediately and arrived in a short time with her two daughters. So we decided that we would give them a bit of privacy and we left with the promise from Betty that she would phone us as soon as she could and let us know what was happening. She had spoken to the Doctor who had said that Joe was very dangerously ill, so she immediately phoned for the priest and we left with a very sad heart. When Betty did phone it was to tell us that Joe had died in the early hours of the morning after he had received the last sacraments from the priest. She said that at the moment Joe died there was a wonderful feeling of peace and serenity filling the room. The priest felt it also and said to Betty. 'I am sure you would not want to bring him back to suffer any more'. Although Betty's heart was breaking she slowly shook her head. I have heard it said that the people know when their end is near and I think that in holding my hand Joe was saying his goodbye to me.

In less than four short years I had lost four members of my family, and now there was only Chris and I left.

John loved his game of golf and he and a friend played regularly once a week but after a while he found with the arthritis in his knees it was very tiring for him and so he switched to playing bowls which was easier and joined the Grampian's bowls club. After a while he became quite a good player and even won a shield at one of their competitions of which he was very proud. He was still working in the school as a technician and life was settling down again but cruel fate had not quite finished with us yet. In 1989 we had been for a week's holiday in Cornwall but on the return journey we were caught in a traffic jam which lasted for hours. We could not move in either direction and the red light came on to let us know the engine was overheating but there was nothing we could do as we were trapped in a line of traffic so could not move either way or stop to let the engine cool down, it was a nightmare journey and I could see that John was getting very worried and anxious but thankfully at last there was a break in the traffic and he managed to get off that road. We had left Cornwall just after breakfast about 10am and eventually arrived home about 2am the following morning. This was on the Saturday morning and John felt unwell the whole of the weekend and went to see the doctor on the Monday and was told he had suffered a heart attack and was immediately rushed into hospital where he spent a few days before being sent home again. In the following months he had a few recurring chest pains which meant more time spent in hospital and on one of his visits the doctor told him that he would have to go to London to see a surgeon who was one of the top specialists in the field of heart surgery as it was thought he would need a bypass operation. They laid on a car to take him to

London the same day and when he saw the specialist he said that he would have to have a triple bypass operation as soon as possible. This was in November 1990 and they decided that the operation would take place on the 13th November which was in 2 days time. John was a bit worried about the date although he was not really superstitious. However, as it happened there was a hold up somewhere down the line and it could not be done on that day. It would now be the following day, the 14th, so that made him feel a little better about it.

As he would be in the hospital in London for quite a while his daughter Ann and I decided we would go there and rent a room to be near him. We arrived at the London Chest Hospital and one of the nurses told us that the minister of the church next door sometimes let out rooms in the church for anyone who had relations in the hospital. So we went to see him and got a room which was vacant at that time. It was not exactly a first class hotel but at least we would be close to John and that was the main thing. The Minister informed us that it would cost £6 a night for the room, so we booked it for a week. It was a very cheerless and bare place with just a bed and few bits of furniture and there was a little gas fire in the room which the minister told us not to use unless it was absolutely necessary. When he had gone we inspected the bed. The sheets and blankets were clean but felt damp, so we stripped it and dried everything in front of the gas fire and made sure they were dry before making up the bed again. We thought that was a necessity unless we wanted to catch pneumonia from the damp sheets and anyway, what the minister did not know would not hurt him.

We knew exactly where John's ward window was and we could wave good night to him before we went to bed and, of course, visit him during the day. So it made all the difference to him and to us that we were so close.

During the day our lodgings were fine as we had each other for company and there was always something going on in the church hall, but at night when the door was locked at 10 o'clock we were on our own again. The toilet was at the far end of the corridor so if one of us had to pay a visit it meant that the other one had to go too as we were scared to go on our own.

I have heard before that the Cockney people were very hospitable and this was the East End of London where most of them are of that breed, and we found this to be true. Everyday there was a cheap lunch laid on for the pensioners of the parish and although we were not in that category, the people insisted that we took our meal with them and paid the same price as they did. They were a lovely crowd of people and made us so welcome and we owe them a big debt of gratitude for their generosity.

John was in the hospital for a week and he could not have been in a better place as he was so well cared for. The food was wonderful, well cooked and piping hot and the care he received was first class. The sister of the ward was a lovely person and cared only for the wellbeing of the patients in her care. John kept in touch with the sister for months after he returned home. Mary his youngest daughter worked in the Avon factory at that time and the workers there were allowed to buy a bag of cosmetics at a very cheap price and John used to buy them from her and send them to the hospital to use for raffle prizes etc. on their open day that was held to raise money for the upkeep of the hospital.

On the 21st November John was 65 years of age and we had to celebrate his birthday in the hospital. Not exactly the way we had planned it but at least he was on the way to recovery and that was all that mattered. On the last night of our stay I asked Ann to take the rent that was due for our stay in the church hall to the minister. She returned about half an hour later grinning all over her face. I asked her what was amusing her and she burst out laughing and said, 'The minister tried to get fresh with me', and I gasped in amazement saying, 'What did you do?' She said, 'I just said 'is that your wife coming back already?" The minister gave her a terrified glance and scuttled from the room like a scared rabbit. Ann was a big girl in every way and had nothing to fear from him and if it had come to a wrestling match I know who I would have put my money on, and it would not have been the randy vicar. But it just shows that you can't trust anyone these days.

When John got home the welfare branch of his union arranged for him to have a brief stay at their convalescent home in Llandudno and the restful break away made all the difference to his health. So when he finally came home he was more or less back to his normal self, although he had been warned not to lift anything heavy or get stressed in any way. Now that he had reached retiring age he gave up his job at the school and settled down to a less strenuous life.

Chapter 20

It is now 2011. I am 87 years of age and my young sister Chris is aged 82. So I guess now we are both living on borrowed time. Chris was not as fortunate as I was, as her husband died very suddenly in 1990, although he had not been in the best of health for some time. Chris has now been on her own for over 20 years and although it is a very lonely life sometimes, she copes very well.

I have been fortunate that I still have John with me. I am not afraid of growing old with all the aches and pains that come with advancing years and the senses being less sharp than they were, but what I do miss is waking up in the morning and looking forward to the new day ahead. When you are young each day is an adventure, a blank page ready to be filled and written on. Now there are no more pages to work on and I know that each day is going to be more or less exactly what it was the day before and probably the following day also. It is the sameness of life now that I find most depressing, never looking forward always looking back. On looking back on my own life I know that I have been very fortunate; a happy childhood with devoted parents, a good and loyal family around me, and when the road became bumpy always a good friend to smooth the path. I was never going to set the world afire with any deeds of mine but there is one thing that I am rather proud of and that is that I brought up a son of whom any mother would be proud. Clever, yes, and at the top of his profession, but more importantly with a kind and a sensitive nature.

The road through life is not easy for anyone and sometimes it has been very chilly for June, but just occasionally in the dark drear days of winter the sun will suddenly shine through, reminding us that winter won't last forever and spring is just around the corner. I may not have done anything extraordinary in my life but I have been fortunate to witness some amazing events that have changed our lives.

The 1939 - 1945 War, when Britain was left on her own to face the might of the seemingly invincible German army, with only the spirit of the British people and a stretch of water standing between us and defeat, but we were victorious against all the odds. I was here at the birth of space travel which ended with a man setting foot on the surface of the moon. The advent of television which brought mass entertainment into every family home. And the electronic age when mobile phones and computers are available and any information that you require can be found on the internet at the press of a button, and now these articles can be found in almost every home.

To me it seems only like yesterday but in reality it was fifty years ago when we stood watching the crowd of dancers on the floor and my friend said something to me that I have never forgotten: *'These are all just ordinary people with ordinary mundane lives but everyone of these has a story to tell'*. And this is mine.

www.ingramcontent.com/pod-product-compliance
Lightning Source LLC
Chambersburg PA
CBHW072121020426
42334CB00018B/1672